MW01379391

DREAMS DO COME TRUE

A LIFELONG YANKEES FAN VISITS THE STADIUM

#14
Vern - to my good friend
and Coronado teammate, and
U.S. Coast Guard veteran —
Lots of good memories.
Thanks for serving our country,
and being a friend.
Go Cougars,
Ron Bontrager #12

DREAMS DO COME TRUE

A LIFELONG YANKEES FAN VISITS THE STADIUM

RON BONTRAGER

TATE PUBLISHING
AND ENTERPRISES, LLC

Dreams Do Come True: A Lifelong Yankees Fan Visits the Stadium
Copyright © 2016 by Ron Bontrager. All rights reserved.

No part of this publication may be reproduced, stored in a retrieval system or transmitted in any way by any means, electronic, mechanical, photocopy, recording or otherwise without the prior permission of the author except as provided by USA copyright law.

The opinions expressed by the author are not necessarily those of Tate Publishing, LLC.

Published by Tate Publishing & Enterprises, LLC
127 E. Trade Center Terrace | Mustang, Oklahoma 73064 USA
1.888.361.9473 | www.tatepublishing.com

Tate Publishing is committed to excellence in the publishing industry. The company reflects the philosophy established by the founders, based on Psalm 68:11,

"The Lord gave the word and great was the company of those who published it."

Book design copyright © 2016 by Tate Publishing, LLC. All rights reserved.
Cover design by Norlan Balazo
Interior design by Manolito Bastasa

Published in the United States of America

ISBN: 978-1-68207-474-9
1. Sports & Recreation / Baseball / History
2. Sports & Recreation / Baseball / General
16.02.05

To Josh, Lori, and Daniel

*Two young men and one young lady
who play, watch, and enjoy baseball.*

*Maybe one day one of your children
will like the Yankees.*

ACKNOWLEDGMENTS

My trip to New York was exceptional. I traveled alone, but it took the help of numerous friends to get me there. It is the same with this book. There are many I need to thank for their encouragement which has led to the fulfillment of another dream: publishing this book.

I am grateful for the good people at Tate Publishing who took a chance on me and this work.

My daughter Lori made a huge contribution with her editing skills. She read and re-read this material, making numerous corrections and suggestions along the way. I didn't realize I raised a daughter who knew how to help me look so much better.

Ken Miller has been a good friend for many years. He, too, read the manuscript and offered helpful suggestions.

I am indebted to Ron Green, Jr., Maury Allen, Bill Madden, and Phil Pepe, sports writers and authors of excellent books on baseball. They responded to my correspondence and offered words of advice and encouragement before I began writing.

I have enjoyed reading several books during recent years, which is what convinced me that I ought to give this one a try. The books related to baseball history filled me with facts and fascination. They helped me relive the enjoyable years of my childhood. I frequently went back to the information in the books to help me as I wrote this one. My favorite ones are listed on the final pages.

I was helped by www.baseball-reference.com, which provided needed information just as fast as I could click a mouse. I can't imagine how much time, hard work, and fun go into compiling the information on that web site.

Thanks also to the late George Steinbrenner and his family. The Boss was determined to do everything necessary to continue the Yankees tradition of excellence and success so that my grandchildren would have a team in the Bronx to call "Champions."

I have been blessed with three children, all grown up now, and their spouses, with whom I can easily talk baseball and still play catch, and I have satisfaction when we do. They have blessed my wife and me with grandchildren, with whom I hope to continue talking baseball. Our three were nearly as excited as I about my trips to New York and writing this book, even though they won't cheer for the Yankees.

Finally, I am thankful for Bev and the joy it is being married to her. Even though I was going on my dream trip to New York without her, she smiled and assured me of her love when she kissed me and said goodbye at the airport. After reading the first five chapters of this book, she said, "This is good," then added, "You have to find a publisher." She is still "just like a dream come true" to me, more so than anything and everything I have written in this book.

CONTENTS

Preface 13

1. Field of My Dreams 25
2. Going Home 41
3. There is Crying in Baseball 57
4. Always a Yankee 73
5. Team October 95
6. New York, New York 111
7. Playing Center Field in Yankee Stadium 129
8. A Glorious Quest 147
9. Priceless! 165
10. Reliving the Dream 179
11. Reflections on My Cup of Coffee 195

References 207
Recommended Readings 211

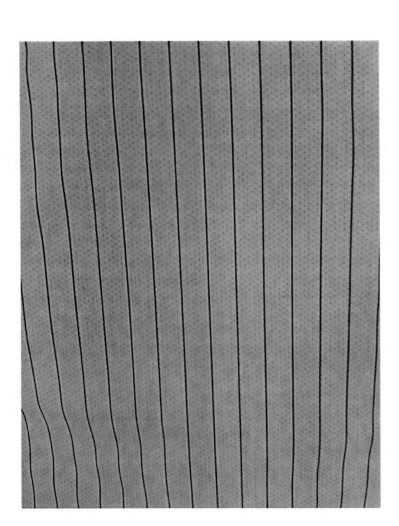

PREFACE

I WENT ONLINE to vote for the greatest moment in Yankee Stadium history. What a disappointment that June 22, 2005, was not on the list. At the very least there should have been a write-in option because that was an extremely important date. It was the day I visited Yankee Stadium.

It was the day my dream came true.

Veni, vidi, vici. Like Julius Caesar, I came, I saw, and I conquered!

Writing this book has been enjoyable, but it hasn't come without several delays and distractions. It has been nearly ten years since the idea was conceived. After my visit to the Stadium, I began to plan every chapter. Writing the first few came easily. Over the next few years, after writing only two or three more chapters, I doubted that this would ever come to print. Now, as a cold winter has passed and spring training has concluded, I have finally seen this project come to birth. It is just in time for a new season—the first in the post-Jeter era.

I like the way Derek Jeter played, from his rookie-of-the-year season in 1996 until his final at bat at Fenway Park eighteen years later. I didn't grow up a Jeter fan, but I understand what it feels like when an icon, one's childhood hero, retires. When I think about baseball my mind often returns to my childhood. I remember the spring of 1969, the first year in the post-Mantle era. I was 15, and I knew I had experienced the last of my special childhood memories of Mickey Mantle with the New York Yankees.

So for all Yankees fans, especially those who cut their teeth while rooting for Mantle or Jeter, this book is for you. In the midst of the delays, the reason for writing has not changed. From the beginning thoughts to the final sentence, I have wanted to tell my story. It is about cheering for the Yankees and dreaming of visiting that exceptional baseball stadium in the South Bronx.

For most of my life, my dream was to journey to Yankee Stadium. The dream finally came true on that cloudy, beginning-of-summer afternoon nearly ten years ago.

I played baseball when I was a boy, and I dreamed of wearing Yankee pinstripes like my hero Mickey Mantle. I desired to wear Number 7, to be a switch hitter, and to play centerfield, until 1967, when I, too, switched to first base. Like so many of my generation, I was a Mantle fan. The Commerce Comet is still my favorite player. I don't think there has ever been a second favorite.

My baseball playing "career" came to an end when I reached high school. I had neither the size nor the ability to play. I didn't have the money to buy new cleats and a new glove, and I didn't want to ask my parents to buy them for me. In addition, I didn't want to face Rick Gossage, the pitcher for our cross-town rival Wasson High School who is now enshrined in the Baseball Hall of Fame in Cooperstown, New York. Gossage was called Rick in Colorado Springs. It wasn't until he signed his initial baseball contract in 1970 with the White Sox that he began going by Rich, and soon after that a friend nicknamed him "Goose."

As things turned out, my final season of organized baseball was in the summer of 1969. Just weeks before men walked on the moon a ball scooted between my legs (it must have been a bad hop in that rocky outfield) and rolled to the fence, ending the game. I walked off the field for what turned out to be the last time I would wear a baseball uniform. So many times I have replayed that ball and rethought my decision to quit playing. Both were mistakes I wish I would not have made. The dream, however, didn't stop then. I still had visions of going to Yankee Stadium.

As a high school sophomore, I took a journalism course because I wanted to be a sports writer. The next year I got a job as a stringer for *The Gazette*, the leading newspaper in Colorado Springs. I continued working for the paper and after graduating high school in 1972, I got a second job

– 15 –

as the announcer/scorer at Memorial Park (once a minor league field, built for the Colorado Springs Sky Sox in the 1950s) for the next three summers. I saw and wrote about many future major leaguers, like Mike Scott, Ron Hassey, and Keith Moreland who played summer ball in Colorado. I was certain I would advance and get a good job in sports journalism and eventually work in the Yankee Stadium press box. That too did not materialize.

After graduating college, my focus on life changed, so I pursued what has become a very enjoyable and satisfying work in Christian ministry. I thought it would be cool to go to the Bronx Cathedral some day and preach "The Sermon on the Mound," although I never really thought that would happen.

Not in pinstripes, not in the press box, and not the Stadium pulpit.

Still the dream lived on. Images of the playing field, the bleachers, Monument Park, and the players had regular meetings in my head. Even though I often thought it would never happen, the dream never died. It took on a new form of reality, called "extremely doubtful," because of low salaries, my children's activities, work obligations, and the recurring phrase, "do the sensible thing, dreamer" that kept running through my mind. I wondered if I would ever fulfill my dream.

In recent years, I worried when I would hear reports about Yankee Stadium being torn down or the Yankees moving to New Jersey. I had determined that if that were to happen, I would be justified in borrowing the money to make the once-in-a-lifetime trip to Yankee Stadium while it was still home to the greatest franchise in sports history. My biggest nightmare was hearing an announcement during the off season that there would be a new home for the Yankees and never another game at the Stadium. My heart goes out to fans of the Brooklyn Dodgers and the New York Giants who heard a similar announcement about their teams moving out of New York. When the Yankees announced plans to build a new stadium, ready for the 2009 season, I had already purchased my game ticket and made my plane reservation. I was going. My dream was about to come true in 2005.

Earlier that year, I had been invited to Albany to preach in October. I had begun saving money for souvenirs, thinking I would be able to see the Stadium and maybe watch a game while I was in New York. But I was discouraged again when I learned there were no tours of Yankee Stadium in October. And if the Yankees were to make it to the playoffs, I doubted there would be a ticket available, or one at an affordable price. What was I to do?

I acted a little irresponsibly, I guess. I was like a boy who wouldn't take no for an answer. I decided that I needed to make two trips from Texas to New York in 2005, which seemed to defy all logic, good sense, and financial responsibility. I accumulated enough money for a game ticket and souvenirs, but I had none to pay for airfare. Besides, there were home improvements to be made, our children's college loans to be paid, and hundreds of more practical ways to spend our money. And most importantly, my dream trip would not include having my sweet wife Bev at my side (or, rather, a few steps behind). We had already planned for her to go with me to Albany and to use the money I received for preaching to pay for her airfare, but there wasn't enough irresponsibility on my part for her to go on this trip, too. I would have to face the consequences of my decision.

Planning the summer trip to New York was one of the most ridiculous and selfish decisions I have ever made. My children were excited, but it didn't settle well with my wife. Was I just fulfilling a childhood fantasy? Was I acting like what so many have said of my gender: we are just boys who never grow up? Bev said I was having a midlife crisis; I said, "Better baseball than a younger woman." Could I really justify the expense? Besides, I would have more than three years before "the House that Ruth built" would be replaced.

Then it struck me. "We're talking baseball, here. It is our national pastime. I have to go, and I have to go now."

The 1970s car commercial was filled with truisms: "They go together, in the good ole USA, baseball [my favorite sport] and hot dogs [is there anything better to eat at a ball game?], apple pie [you wonder about people who don't like apple pie] and Chevrolet [my dad sold Chevys for several years]." I agree with every part of the song.

Americans are tough, rugged people who overcome odds. Manager Jimmy Dugan, played by Tom Hanks in *A League of Their Own*, summed it up well when he said, "There's no crying in baseball." Surely Francis Scott Key had baseball in mind when he wrote "The Star Spangled Banner." It seems to me that our national anthem ends with, "and the home of the brave. Play Ball!"

Even if he didn't *really* invent the game, it is hard to imagine America without Abner Doubleday and his cow pasture in Cooperstown. I still get goose bumps when I hear Terrence Mann, played by James Earl Jones in *Field of Dreams* make his statement about baseball:

> The one constant through all the years, Ray, has been baseball. America has rolled by like an army of steam rollers. It's been erased like a blackboard, rebuilt, and erased again. But baseball is a mark of time. This field, this game, is a part of our past, Ray. It reminds us of all that once was good and could be again.

Just hearing him say "baseball" brings chills up and down my spine. And yes, baseball does remind us of all that is good.

It is fitting that baseball begins in the spring when everything seems to be recovering and hope returns. In my mind (I'm sure it wasn't in George Harrison's), "Here Comes the Sun" is a great song for February; it is about baseball. Some of the lines include, "It's been a long cold lonely winter. It feels like years since it's been here. The smiles [are] returning to the faces. Here comes the sun, and I say, it's alright."

Baseball defines America in many ways. Early in baseball's history, Walt Whitman, a 19th Century American poet, wrote, "I see great things in baseball; it's our game—the American game." Many years later, another great truth was stated by Jacques Barzun, the French-born historian. He was correct when he stated in 1954 (the year I was born), "Whoever would know the mind and heart of America had better learn baseball." Owner and promoter Bill Veeck said, "Baseball is almost the only orderly thing in a very unorderly world. If you get three strikes, even the best lawyer in the world can't get you off."

If I needed anything else, patriotic or otherwise, to convince me that I should go to Yankee Stadium, I didn't know what it could possibly be. This had been my dream for over 40 years. I was certain that the time had come for the dream to come true.

Baseball *is* America. And so much more.

Baseball is the old pros, the early 20th Century players like Ty Cobb, Babe Ruth, Honus Wagner, Walter Johnson, and Christy Mathewson. These original inductees into Baseball's Hall of Fame in 1939 played for the love of the game and excelled as few have since. One of the first books I bought, in grade school, was about those five players. I still have the book and get the same feelings when looking at it today as I did then.

Baseball's history includes pioneers like William Arthur "Candy" Cummings, who claimed he threw the first curveball; Roger Bresnahan, the first catcher to wear shin guards; Branch Rickey, Jackie Robinson, and the game's "great experiment"; and Larry MacPhail who brought night baseball to the major leagues. Baseball has left us with memories of the courage and efforts of men like Lou Gehrig, Satchel Paige, Pete Gray, and Kirk Gibson.

Baseball has its milestones and never-to-be-forgotten moments, like Gehrig's farewell speech, Bobby Thomson's "the Giants win the pennant" home run, Don Larsen's perfect game, Henry Aaron's 715th homer in Atlanta, the Mark McGwire-Sammy Sosa home run battle in 1998, and the Yankee dynasty.

Baseball is numbers. I always think of Mantle when I see the number seven; Mays and 24 go together, as do Jackie Robinson and 42. I was always good in math, partly because I learned how to figure batting averages at an early age. How I love baseball statistics! I grew up knowing the meaning of 511; 2,130, with all respect to Cal Ripken, Jr.;

4,191, sorry Pete, nothing personal; 714, surpassed but not forgotten; and 56. In my youth, I never thought any of those records would fall.

Baseball has its nicknames, like the Bambino and the Sultan of Swat, High Pockets, Wahoo Sam, Poosh 'em Up Tony, School Boy, the Big 6, Dizzy and Daffy, Leo the Lip, Joltin' Joe, Stan the Man, the Splendid Splinter, the Say Hey Kid, Hammerin' Hank, the Ryan Express, and the Goose. And the teams: Murderer's Row and the Bronx Bombers, the Gashouse Gang, the Mackian Maulers, dem Bums, the Amazin' Mets, the Big Red Machine, and Harvey's Wallbangers.

Baseball is a huge part of family life, too. Even though the times were few, I loved every time I played catch with my grandpa Bontrager, and I have fond memories of my dad hitting pop flies to my brother, sisters, and me in our back yard on Sunday afternoons. I enjoyed playing catch with my sons and daughter, and I got a big thrill hitting them pop-ups while they stood at the top of the hill on the seldom-traveled street in front of our Arkansas home. It was a great place for hitting flies: if I hit the ball too far, it rolled back to the kids, and if they made a poor throw, the ball still made it down the hill to me. And the neighbors didn't mind if I hit one in their yard. I intend to continue doing those things with my grandchildren. When I began writing this book I was only a "grandpa-in-waiting," but now I have five special little ones who need to know more about the Yankees because their parents will be telling them to cheer for the Braves.

"Yes!" I decided. "I should make this trip and visit Yankee Stadium, and I should do it now. Why wait until later?" For years I had been trying to cancel my membership in Procrastinators Anonymous. It was the right thing to do.

I am 60 years old; I love my family, I love baseball, and I'm trying to publish my first book, but until I made the plane reservation and bought a ticket for the Yankees' game on June 22, 2005, I had never done a crazy thing in my whole life. Yes, that is a slightly modified comment from the opening scene in my favorite movie, *Field of Dreams*.

It is okay to be crazy once in awhile. We all are in different ways and at different times. Didn't Will Rogers say something like that? I am sure he was a baseball fan, too. After all, he was born in the area now known as Oklahoma, Mickey Mantle's home state.

On June 21, the night before my dream date with Yankee Stadium, the Yanks exploded for thirteen runs in the eighth-inning to beat the Rays, 20-11. I expected even more fireworks on my afternoon at the Stadium. The dream was about to come true. I was about to discover something very special, like the song, "Eye of the Tiger," which includes the words, "Don't lose your grip on the dreams of the past." No grip-loss for me. I was going to Yankee Stadium the next day.

This book is about a man, well maybe it's about a boy who never grew up, who discovered great joy when his dream came true and who also discovered you can never be too old to feel like a child. It is a reflection on life, excitement, anticipation, and a return to boyhood fun and fantasy.

It is for everyone who shares my love for baseball. I really think that even those who despise the Yankees but love America's pastime can relate to what is written here. Maybe it will be an encouragement for others to finally go to a game or to write down their thoughts about baseball. Baseball enthusiasts are part of a fellowship of baseball fanatics who grew up enjoying the game, the numbers, the nicknames, the history, the playing fields, and life lessons we have learned from the game.

That's baseball. That's why I went to New York. And that's why I wrote this book.

Yes, dreams do come true.

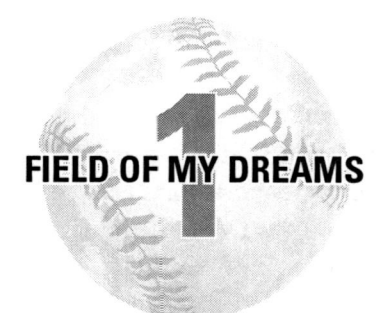

FIELD OF MY DREAMS

"Hey, is this heaven?"

—Shoeless Joe Jackson

THERE WAS A very special place in the Bronx borough of New York City. Located across the Harlem River at 161st Street and River Avenue, it became America's number one sports venue. It was a place where memories were made and dreams came true.

Many called it "The House that Ruth built." He built it, and I came.

My dream of visiting Yankee Stadium lasted more than 40 years. What a joy when the dream came true.

Yankee Stadium, "The Home of Champions," did not disappoint. It was for people of all ages, backgrounds, and even team allegiances who went to that magical place and were touched by its wonder.

Baseball didn't begin there, but neither did George Washington live in the White House. There has been so much history and excitement at these places; they gave people a sense of awe, amazement, and tons of memories. It makes me wonder how people ever survived without them. Now, with a new Yankee Stadium across the street from the field of my dreams, new memories are being made.

Just as the back of card 86 in the Upper Deck Yankees Classics series states, "There may not be a more revered sporting venue in the country than Yankee Stadium. Admired and respected by hosts and visitors alike, the Stadium is a place that has seen some of the greatest moments in baseball history." I think every moment at Yankee Stadium was a great moment in baseball history. Just being there was a great thrill. I won, whether the Yankees won or lost. They lost the game on the day of my visit, but I experienced the thrill of victory.

That was especially true on June 22, 2005. That was the day I made it. My lifelong dream of going there came true. I cannot remember a time when I did not like baseball, when I was not a Yankees fan, or when I did not dream of being in Yankee Stadium. This day was special.

It cost $2.5 million to build Yankee Stadium. The first three-tiered seating area had seats for 60,000 cranks (an early name for those who cheered for their team); it was the first ball field to be called a stadium. The first game played at the

Stadium was April 18, 1923. Babe Ruth hit a three-run home run, and the Yankees beat the Boston Red Sox, 4-1. New York went on to win the World Series that year, its first of many championships. Ruth and the Yankees ushered in significant changes that year. History has identified the Bambino, the Yankees, and the Stadium as the greatest baseball player, sports franchise, and athletic venue in American history.

For 50 years, the Stadium was ideal for Yankees baseball as well as football, boxing, and other activities. In the late 60s, re-modeling or destruction, perish the thought, were the only two options for the Stadium. Fortunately, the former was chosen, and for two years, 1974–75, the Yankees played baseball in Shea Stadium while Yankee Stadium improvements were underway.

Finally, on April 15, 1976, the Yankees went back home and won the initial game played at the refurbished house that Ruth built. It was an 11-4 victory over the Minnesota Twins. Like the inaugural season at the Stadium, New York also won the pennant and went to the World Series that year, our nation's bicentennial. It was the first time the Yankees made it to the Series since that very special year of 1964. There had been eleven dark Octobers, and the winning tradition had returned. After losing that Series to the Reds, the Yankees gained the next two titles.

Memories have been made at Yankee Stadium. So many of them! Yankee teams have thrilled their fans with thousands of victories: 27 World Series championships, out-standing performances like Don Larsen's perfect game in the 1956 Series and Roger Maris' 61st home run in 1961, and emotional events like Lou Gehrig's "luckiest man on the face of the earth" speech on July 4, 1939 and the Babe's farewell comments eight years later.

There have been a few heartbreaking losses in the Bronx, like on my visit when the Yanks lost 5-3 to Tampa Bay, but for baseball fans—all the boys and girls who grew up to be men and women, cheering for their favorite teams—and especially Yankees fans, attending a game at Yankee Stadium has to be one of baseball's greatest treasures. Like Ruth on that April day in 1923, I knocked a home run on that Wednesday afternoon.

My earliest memories of a Yankee season go back to 1964, the last year of the dynasty that included ten champi-onships in 15 World Series appearances during an 18-year period that began in 1947. I was ten years old in 1964. Mickey Mantle was my favorite player, and I checked the sports pages every day during the season. I also played organized baseball for the first time that summer in the 9-10 year old division of Colorado Springs' "Old Timers Association" league. My first team was sponsored by the Centennial Sertoma Club of Colorado Springs. We were given a red cap and white t-shirts with red letters. My baseball card collecting began that year also. My greatest desire then was to play baseball with Mickey Mantle and the Yankees at Yankee Stadium.

Two parts of that dream never happened, but the other finally did. It took more than 40 years, but the wait was worth it.

At age 51, I was acting and thinking like that ten-year-old boy I used to be. I didn't need any caffeine to raise my excitement level. The adrenaline was maxing out. I was pumped.

The day finally arrived! I wore a Babe Ruth Cooperstown Collection jersey, which was given to me by one of my students, and a Yankees hat—one of the first I had purchased in 1994 when I began collecting hats of all major league teams. I had pictures, baseballs, and other items that I hoped to get autographed. I also took a score book that I received in 1972 when I joined the National Baseball Congress' Scorers Association. It's the same one I took with me to Comiskey Park when I saw the Yankees play two games against Rick Gossage and the White Sox.

With great excitement I got on the B-train in downtown Manhattan. After several stops, I finally made it to the place where millions have exited on their way to the Stadium. There was so much anticipation as I rushed to leave the 161st Street exit. I climbed the stairs, walked outside, and then, as John Madden would say, "Boom!" There it was, the field of my dreams. I was not disappointed.

The weather was nearly perfect for a game of baseball in the afternoon. There were a few clouds, a pleasant breeze, and a very comfortable temperature of 75 degrees. I had prayed for a clear day, and even though there was a light rain in the 9th inning, it wasn't enough to stop the game or dampen my spirits.

Goose Gossage also grew up a Yankees fan in Colorado Springs. The big difference between his and my youth was that he had "Star" written all over his future, which included induction into baseball's Hall of Fame in 2008. The dream of playing in Yankee Stadium, shared by both him and his father, was always a strong possibility. He was not yet 21 when his dream came true in 1972. In his autobiography, he described his initial visit to the Stadium with these words:

> One of the highlights of [my rookie] season was making my first trip to Yankee Stadium. I jumped off the bus when we arrived at the stadium, and while my teammates went to the clubhouse to dress for the game, I dashed up to a security guard and asked for directions to the field. Then I raced down a corridor...what a sight to behold. Yankee Stadium, the greatest citadel in sports.

The Goose gave an accurate description. Yankee Stadium was, indeed, a citadel of sports.

"The Citadel" is the name of the first large shopping mall that opened in our home town of Colorado Springs. It is huge; multitudes of people go there. The citadel the Goose referred to in the Bronx was also huge and full of people. In 2005, over 4 million fans, which is nearly 50,000 per game, went through the Stadium turnstiles. I was fortunate enough to be one of them.

I flew into Newark on Monday that week and stayed with a former student, Adam Husdon and his wife Maybelle. Adam was the preacher in nearby Bridgewater. He knew I wanted to go to Yankee Stadium, and when he moved there, he offered me a place to stay anytime I was in the area.

Tuesday was a busy day for me. I got up early to go into the City. I took a tour of Manhattan, walked around Times Square, and went up the Empire State Building. I also went in the Chrysler Building, hoping to go to the YES Network offices, but I wasn't allowed on the elevator. I took many pictures and did some shopping at Macy's and Modell's, where I bought Braves shirts for my children. My favorite store was the Yankees Clubhouse on 42nd Street.

Eventually, I took the subway to the Lincoln Center and walked to the ABC Studios for an audition with "Who Wants to be a Millionaire." It was my favorite game show, and I had been trying for five years to be a contestant. I would not have gone for an audition unless I could also see

Yankee Stadium. I got to do both. The latter part of June 2005 would go down in my life's story as a very significant time.

I returned to Bridgewater in time to see the last few innings of Tuesday's game with Tampa Bay. Things didn't look good for the Yankees until the eighth inning. It was the first day of summer, the longest day of the year, and a long night for the Rays. They had knocked Randy Johnson out of the game after three innings, roughing him up for seven runs on eight hits, including three homers. They went back on the field for the eighth, leading 11-7, and they stayed in the field a long, long time.

When the inning finally ended, New York had scored 13 runs and went on to win, 20-11. I was hoping for even more excitement when I went to the Stadium the next day. I called home to speak with Bev and then got ready for bed. I had so much on my mind that falling asleep was quite a challenge. I couldn't wait to get up in the morning and leave. I was going to Yankee Stadium!

I left early for the train ride from Bridgewater to Penn Station in Manhattan. I ascended the stairs, surveyed Madison Square Garden, and then hurried the few blocks to the Manhattan Mall station where I caught the B train on its way to the Bronx. In a short time, I was at the 161st Street exit, about three hours before game time. The boy in me took over from there.

I immediately saw the massive walls beyond left field, my first visual of the place I had desired to see for over 40 years. Memories began to fill my mind, not just of the things that happened inside but also of things that I had imagined happening.

There was a truck entrance where I could survey part of the seating on the first base side. I stood there for about ten minutes. The light blue colored seats were beautiful. I walked toward the front of the Stadium, letting my eyes see as much as possible. There were small groups of people scattered around and boys playing baseball on a field across the street. What a thrill that must be, too, playing baseball beside Yankee Stadium. I'm sure many were hoping for autographs and probably some of them were also excited about seeing their first game there. I just figured that I was the happiest fan of all, just to be at that spot on God's beautiful earth. I was there, enjoying every minute of it, and I was still on the outside.

As I walked farther along, a security person told me to stop. I thought, "What have I done? I'm just an innocent kid who means no harm." I was about to enter the restricted area, a place only for players, team officials, media, special guests, and other privileged individuals. I turned and began walking to the other side of the Stadium—until I got to the restricted area on that side. Again I peered in and saw the bleachers on the first base side. As I continued, I saw

— 33 —

concessions, ticket areas, parking, excited fans, and "the bat." The bat is the former smoke stack that had become the meeting place since the Stadium was remodeled in the mid-1970s. It was an icon in front of *the* icon.

I saw where the "elite" got to drive through, park their cars, and enter the Stadium. I thought to myself that I could have been one of them if my life had traveled a different path. I stood there with many others who were hoping to see a player and get an autograph, but I figured all the Yankees had entered the Stadium already, since their batting practice was to begin in a few minutes, although they didn't need it after the previous night's barrage of hits. I walked a short distance from the Stadium and took some pictures of the front entrance, which was filled with banners of the championship years.

While I was waiting for 11:05 a.m. (entrance into the Stadium was not permitted to the fans until two hours before game time), Tampa Bay's bus arrived. Manager Lou Piniella was one of the first ones off the bus. The man next to me yelled, "Hey Lou, what happened last night?" I'm sure he was a Yankees fan wanting a repeat of the previous night's game.

I worked my way back toward the area where I would enter the Stadium (my seat was on the third base side) and waited for the gate to open. I knew it wouldn't be long.

My sister Carol is not a Yankees fan. Her two favorite teams have always been the Dodgers and whoever was playing the Yankees. Carol, our three siblings, and I were born in Iowa. Four of us were born in Iowa City, near that cornfield-turned-baseball diamond that was made popular in the movie, *Field of Dreams*. She went there once and walked on the field. She grabbed a bat, took a few swings, and sat in the wooden bleachers. She has pictures of that field. I have pictures of Yankee Stadium. I like mine better.

Yankee Stadium, June 22, 2005

	1	2	3	4	5	6	7	8	9	R	H	E
Tampa Bay	0									0	1	0
Yankees	2									2	2	0

Carl Pavano had barely finished his warm-up tosses before he lost his no-hitter to Rays' left-fielder Carl Crawford, who slapped the game's first pitch for a single. Pitching from the stretch, Pavano sat down the next three batters on strikes. Crawford had stolen second, but he was stranded there as his teammates couldn't connect on Pavano's fastballs, which were consistently crossing the plate in the low 90s.

When the Yankees came to bat, Derek Jeter grounded out; then Bernie Williams hit a single to left. The night before, Gary Sheffield had two home runs and seven runs batted in. When he followed Williams with his 13th homer, it seemed that the previous night's onslaught was back. The next Yankee run, however, would have to wait. Alex Rodriguez was called out on strikes, and Hideki Matsui grounded out to end the inning.

I had just watched my first inning from the seats of beautiful Yankee Stadium. The Yankees led 2-0, and I was riding high. I wasn't in heaven, but that was about as good as it gets on earth.

My Favorite Yankee Pitchers

My favorite Yankee pitcher in my early years was Whitey Ford, a Hall of Famer who finished his career as one of the Yankees' all-time best hurlers. His lifetime win-loss record of 236-106 (a .690 winning percentage) is the fifth best in baseball history. In World Series games, "The Chairman of the Board" holds eight career records, including most wins (10) and strikeouts (94); he also threw a record 33 consecutive shutout innings.

Ford's all-around toughness defied his physique. He was not big, and he didn't throw real hard, but he got the job done. He was an overachiever. He had the courage and the savvy (and he knew how to doctor the ball) to face opposing batters with great success. I admire him because he overcame many odds while reaching greatness. Some athletes have great talent and do great things; some don't have great talent but still do great things. I will always prefer the latter.

I was only six years old, so I don't remember the 1960 World Series. But Mickey Mantle could never forget it. He cried afterwards. It was the only time, he said, that the better team lost. Whitey Ford did not pitch until game 3. He only started two games and was not available for game 7. Why "Slick" didn't pitch that game is one of the biggest wonders of Yankee baseball during the Casey Stengel era. What was he thinking?

New York got a huge lift on August 10, 1964, when Mel Stottlemyer was called up from Richmond. He had gone 13-3 before joining the Yankees, who were in third place, three and one-half games out. He won his first start and finished the season with nine in 12 decisions, helping the Yankees grab their fifth straight AL pennant. Then he won the pivotal Game 2 against Bob Gibson in the Series and started two other games. I immediately liked the guy. Maybe it was because his name, like mine, was long, and there was a brief time when my friends called me Stottletrigger. I followed his career, most of which was played during a period when the Yankees spent 11 straight years at home in October. Stottlemyer was the ace of the Yankees staff during most of his career. He won 20 or more games three times, each on teams that finished no higher than fifth place. It is sad that he never pitched in another World Series.

I saw Stottlemyer pitch one afternoon in Chicago in 1972. I had gone there hoping to watch the rookie, Rich Gossage, pitch. (I did see him pitch, and he got the win in the game the night before Stottlemyer's start.) I got close to the warm-up area and took a few pictures of Stottlemyer. In the fifth inning, he singled and drove in a run. He was a lifetime .160 hitter; he had seven home runs. He pitched well that afternoon, but the Yankees didn't help him much. Trailing 3-1, he was replaced by a pinch hitter during a Yankees rally in the seventh.

I saw Rick Gossage play basketball when he was at Wasson High School. He was a tall, skinny kid, a real fighter, who was tough under the basket on both ends of the floor. I never saw him pitch in high school, but I had heard about him. He could throw heat! Only the ignorant and foolish stepped in against him without fear. He rarely gave up a hit, and he beaned a lot of batters. He struck out many, and walked almost as many. He needed fine tuning, and he got it with the White Sox.

After just one full year in the minors at Class A Appleton, where he was 18-2 and the MVP in 1971, Chicago brought him to the "show" and soon gave him the name "Goose." I met him after his rookie season and talked to him just long enough to tell him my name, my work at the paper, and that I had seen him pitch in Chicago. He was gracious, and I wished him luck. He had what it took to be a top-notch pitcher and proved he was just that in a 22 year big league career.

I enjoyed reading about him during his next few years with the White Sox where he made the AL all-star team twice and led the league in saves in 1975 and the outstanding 1977 season with the Pirates. Then on November 22, 1977, he signed with the Yankees. I was excited that I knew someone who would be playing for my favorite team. I knew he would be a star.

During those six years with the Yankees, he was tremendous, helping the team to three postseason appearances and winning a World Series. From 1975 to 1985, he was probably the most effective and most feared relief pitcher in the majors. It could be argued that no one in major league history "owned the mound" the way he did during that stretch.

It was a well deserved honor when he entered the Hall of Fame in the summer of 2008, but it's strange to me that it took so long.

Other pitchers to wear pinstripes who have inspired me are David Cone, Andy Pettitte, and Mariano Rivera. I like Coney's personality. He was a fighter, the guy you wanted on the mound during the really tough situations when you had to have an out. He attained perfection: 27 up and 27 down, in a game at the Stadium on July 18, 1999.

I liked Pettitte because of his stare, his unshaven face, and his great move to first. In his rookie season, he was part of the Yankees return to prominence when they entered the 1995 postseason for the first time since 1981. He was on five World Series championship teams from 1996–2009. Although he left the Yankees to play in Houston for three years, he came back and retired as a Yankee.

Rivera, the last major leaguer to wear number 42, was just plain awesome, both as a pitcher and as a person. He made a bad pitch that hurt the team about as often as someone hits an inside-the-park home run these days. He finished his career as the all-time leader in saves with 652. The "Sandman" had a special exit on his final day as a Yankee. When Jeter and Pettitte were sent by manager Joe Girardi to take Rivera out of the game, it became one of the most emotional events in modern-day baseball.

GOING HOME

*"When the Lord brought back the captive ones of Zion,
We were like those who dream."*

—Psalm 126:1

A DREAM IS more than just a desire; it is also the stimulus for pursuing its fulfillment. My dream continued for a long time. When I entered and viewed the inside of the Stadium—the light blue bleachers, the dark green grass, the rich brown dirt in the infield and around the warning track, and the monuments—and also looked at the fans and eventually the players, there was no more dreaming. Reality is so much better. I was there, finally, with so many others wearing Yankee clothing and filled with pinstripe memories and excitement. It was a colossal family reunion.

I felt like I was at home, that I belonged at the Stadium. When I passed through security and the gate on the third base side, I was only a few steps from the diamond. It was my first time there, but I had been there before, so many times before. Everything seemed so comfortable. Like Goldilocks' famous words, it was *just right*. I knew this was "home sweet home." It was better than all of my previous visits through television, newspapers, books, and dreaming during classes in elementary and junior high school.

All of it was first-time new, but it was very familiar, too. It reminded me of John Denver's "Rocky Mountain High," which begins with these seemingly paradoxical words: "He was born in the summer of his 27th year, comin' home to a place he'd never been before." I had often wondered how you can come home to a place you had never been before. When I stood near the field, I knew. Until that June 22 morning, I was on my way; when I arrived at Yankee Stadium, I had made it home.

A welcome mat had been placed there for me. Some may say New Yorkers are mean, rude and would just as likely rob you as look at you. John "Off His" Rocker was wrong. He and I witnessed two different places. I was treated with nothing but kindness throughout my visit there, walking around Manhattan, going in the stores, eating pizza at Café Fiorello (located across from the Lincoln Center; I wanted to eat at the place claiming to serve the best pizza in New York), even riding the subway, and especially watching baseball at Yankee Stadium. Going there was a lot like going to

– 42 –

see my parents and siblings who always treat me special. Being there was like going to church and seeing brothers and sisters with whom I share God's wonderful blessings. I have never paid money to enter family houses or church buildings like I did before entering the Stadium, but I still felt a sense of belonging when I arrived. I was home again, and for the first time, all at the same time.

All the sights, the sounds, the people, and the activity were inspirational. I enjoyed being outside the Stadium for an hour, walking and looking in while the excitement escalated. About 11:05 a.m., it was surreal when I finally got to go in. No more dreaming. No more waiting. The dream had come true. I was on the inside, looking at paradise, agreeing with Chris Jennison who called it "the greatest baseball palace in the world."

Many before me have also spoken of Yankee Stadium with deep respect for both its physical features and the events that have taken place there. Oriole star Cal Ripken, Jr. said, "When I come here, it's like standing on hallowed ground." Former Yankee David Cone, who pitched a perfect game there, called it "the cathedral of baseball" and another former Yankee pitcher, Randy Johnson, described it with two simple and profound words: "Baseball heaven." Yogi Berra said, "Walking into Yankee Stadium for the first time, I felt like I was walking into something from the Bible." Hall of Famer and former Detroit Tiger George

Kell said, "I was in awe of this place. It was almost like one of the great landmarks of the world."

Goose Gossage wrote about being called in from the bullpen to pitch for the first time in Yankee Stadium; he said, "I didn't stride to the mound at my normally rapid clip. I actually dallied. For once I felt in no hurry to rare back and fire. I was too busy taking in the sights of Yankee Stadium, every bit as beautiful as a Rocky Mountain sunset."

Sometimes there is the fear factor of playing at Yankee Stadium. Hank Aaron, who broke Babe Ruth's home run record in 1974, played there for the first time in 1957. "I was scared to death the first time we played here…not so much about the Yankees themselves but frightened of Yankee Stadium and the mystique of playing in the house that Ruth built."

There was another Yankees World Series opponent who spoke highly of the Stadium. Nearly 40 years after Aaron's initial visit, the Braves again faced the Yankees. Greg Maddux and his Atlanta team lost the Series-ending game 6 in the Bronx. The four-time Cy Young winner said, "Obivously it hurts losing, but the atmosphere here is matched nowhere. It's exciting to be out there on the mound…it's wild. Even though we lost, in a while we're going to appreciate being in this place."

When I finally entered through the outer corridor and strolled down the ramp, I was only slightly elevated above the playing field, near the third base dugout. I was stunned as I thought about all the players who have been there. I took a long look around the field and surveyed the bleachers. I was in no hurry to move; I wanted to take it all in.

Memories overwhelmed me like raging flood waters. I could see some of the Stadium's history much more clearly. Seeing where so many outstanding plays took place seemed better than how I remembered them. It was easy to picture Mickey Mantle rounding third, running with his head down, and being met by Frankie Crosetti after hitting another homer. Scenes of the 1964 season, culminating with the World Series, sped through my mind. All of the excitement of a ten-year old Yankees fan came back easily. I felt a sense of pride, remembering that Goose Gossage played here. The final out of the 1996 World Series happened very close to where I stood. With both excitement and sobriety, I remembered those two ninth-inning, two-out, two-run home runs in back-to-back games of the 2001 World Series. I tried to imagine what that day must have felt like for New Yorkers who were just seven weeks removed from the terrorist attacks.

It was difficult to walk away from that spot, but I anticipated seeing other areas. I hustled to find the area with the retired numbers and monuments. The people walked slowly and spoke softly, almost as if visiting a cemetery. The feelings in that place contain both excitement and reverence.

Like all memorials, this area generates respect, honor, and gratitude for those who are remembered.

Each number brought back memories of my childhood when I was reading and watching television. First was Gehrig's Number 4, then the Babe's, followed by Joe D., the Mick (I had to have a picture of me in front of Number 7), and the Ol Perfesser, manager Casey Stengel. Then there were the catchers: Bill Dickey, Yogi Berra, Thurman Munson and Elston Howard with Whitey Ford in the middle. These were followed by Roger Maris, Phil Rizzuto, Billy Martin, Reggie Jackson, Don Mattingly, and Ron Guidry. In the new Stadium, manager Joe Torre and reliever Mariano Rivera have had their numbers retired. Jackie Robinson's number is also there—not because he was a Yankee but because of his contribution to baseball. There is no doubt that Derek Jeter's Number 2 will be next.

Beyond the numbers were the monuments. The first three to greet me were the ones that had previously been on the playing field. There were the tall granite stones honoring Gehrig, Miller Huggins, and Ruth. Behind them on each side were Mantle and DiMaggio. Like many others ahead of me, I asked a fan to take a picture of me in front of Mantle's monument. I heard a young boy ask if the men were buried there. Really, I heard it. As a boy, Bob Costas thought the same thing until being told otherwise. I am sure it happens often.

Dreams Do Come True: A Lifelong Yankees Fan Visits the Stadium

The author in Monument Park at Yankee Stadium

After leaving the monuments, I began my trip around the Stadium. By this time several Tampa Bay players were on the field warming up and getting ready to take batting practice. A few Yankees were on the field, too. I tried to get near the Yankees' dugout, but spectators weren't allowed there without having a ticket for that section. Farther down the first base line, a small but increasing crowd of autograph-seekers was gathering.

With no Yankees nearby, I decided it was better to walk than to wait. I had only taken a few steps when I noticed pitching coach Mel Stottlemyer on his way out to the bull-

– 47 –

pen with one of his pitchers. I had to take a picture to compare it with the ones I have of him warming up before a game at Comiskey Park in 1972.

I ascended to the top row of Yankee Stadium and sat directly behind home plate. What an awesome sight. I had to catch my breath because it is a steep incline and a little difficult for someone with bad feet who gets a little queasy in high places. I studied the vastness of the Stadium and the buildings beyond it. More memories flooded my head.

I took several pictures and made some phone calls. It was a thrill to tell my whereabouts to some of my colleagues in Lubbock. They asked about the previous day's audition, which saddened them upon hearing that I didn't make it. I wasn't the least bit sad about it because the audition was just preliminary to the main event. The time had come, and I was home, feeling like I was on top of the world, at Yankee Stadium.

I descended to the lower sections of the Stadium and started searching for my seat. I wanted to make sure that it was truly there, reserved just for me on that day, but I wasn't ready to sit down yet because I had to continue my journey around the Stadium. I returned to the left field seating area and gathered with others who were hoping to get a batting practice ball. Several were hit there, but none were close enough to me, which was okay because I wasn't there to get BP balls hit by Tampa Bay players. I took another glance at Monument Park, reminisced about some of my favorite players and memories, and then started back toward my seat.

I then decided to go to the concession stand. The line wasn't very long, but I still had this horrible thought: what if I'm still in this line when the game begins? I was a little nervous, but like most anxiety, it was unnecessary. I ordered a huge soft drink and a foot long hot dog. I experienced the truth of actor Humphrey Bogart's words: "A hot dog at the ballpark is better than a steak at the Ritz." I also bought a copy of *Yankees Magazine*, the monthly program. I sat down in what I thought was my seat: section M16, row H, seat 22. It was a tight squeeze, but just as I got comfortable, an usher, a man, and a young boy asked to see my ticket. I was sitting in the wrong seat. I was in section M14. I was a little embarrassed, and I thought how scared I would have been if I were that boy and someone was in my seat. I almost cried because I *was* that boy for that entire day, and I wouldn't have wanted anyone to take my place.

When I got to section M16, I was pleasantly surprised. It was a perfect fit with much more space in front and on the right side. It was the end seat in the last row of the lower section. There was an aisle to my left, and on my right, there was a pillar that protruded just enough so that there wasn't room for a seat. I got all the room at the end of the row, plus this open space on the other side of my seat. My row and about six rows in front of mine were covered by the loge boxes in the second deck. I realized that no foul balls would make it to me, at least not on the fly, but I would be protected from direct sunlight or rain. I had plenty of room to put my things, to relax, and to stretch out.

I could just as well have been at home sitting in my recliner, snacking on chips, reading my magazine between innings, and watching the Yankees on television, but I couldn't have been any more comfortable then I was, sitting in Yankee Stadium.

I had felt right at home in Yankee Stadium for three hours, and then the magazine confirmed it. Right there, on page 82 of the June edition of *Yankees Magazine,* was my name. Really. Sort of. The magazine had an article about several Yankees and their favorite sports off the diamond. Jorge Posada's was cycling, and the magazine had a picture of Lance Armstrong riding in the Tour de France. Armstrong's Trek bikes have several Bontrager wheel parts on them, and the name is easy to see in the picture. (Keith Bontrager is my distant cousin; he has been building bicycles and bike accessories in California since 1980.)

Anticipation continued to mount as the minutes got closer to the 1:05 start time. Then I heard "the Voice." Since 1951, the Yankee Stadium announcer has been Bob Sheppard. Mickey Mantle said he was always moved when he heard, "The center-fielder, number 7, Mickey Mantle."

I remember hearing those words, and the ovation that followed, on television.

When I started announcing baseball games, I would say the name of the batter and the next two. The major league way is to announce only the batter who's coming to the plate, and no one did it better than Bob Sheppard. After hearing it done that way at Comiskey Park in 1972, I changed the way I introduced the batters, and I endured a little criticism for it too. Maybe some parents wanted to hear their son's name mentioned three times before they came to the plate.

A few minutes passed, the players' names were announced, and the Yankees started taking the field. I was about to watch the first pitch of a game at Yankee Stadium. "Hold on, Ronnie," I thought to myself. "This is Christmas day and I'm opening the best present ever."

The internet is a wonderful, inexpensive way to follow baseball. As a young Yankees fan in the 60s, I would wake up early on summer mornings and want to go back to sleep. Then I would remember that the morning paper would be on our front porch, and I could go read about the Yankees. Upstairs I would run, open the front door, grab the paper, and turn to the sports section. I don't have to wait so long anymore. I can go online and follow the game pitch-by-pitch, see the box score, check the standings and statistics, and read about tomorrow's pitchers. I really enjoy the

Yankees site; in fact www.yankees.com is my home page, and I view it often. It is a good thing, to go home.

For years the significance of the shape of home plate had escaped me. How I missed it all those years I'll never know. To look at home plate is to look at a house, and everyone knows the goal of baseball is to go home, to get safely home as many as possible on your team. There is something wonderful about going home.

Yankee Stadium, June 22, 2005

	1	2	3	4	5	6	7	8	9	R	H	E
Tampa Bay	0	0								0	1	0
Yankees	2	0								2	2	0

Carl Pavano continued to impress me by opening the second inning with his fourth straight K. After two infield grounders, the Yankees ran off the field to their dugout.

"For the Yankees in the bottom of the second: no runs, no hits, no errors, and no one left on base." The Yankees were still up 2-0, and everything was looking good.

What a day for a Yankees fan. It was a beautiful afternoon in the House that Ruth Built, and I was watching baseball—Yankees baseball no less—at the field of my dreams.

My Favorite Yankee Catchers

Two catchers who have worn pinstripes have their number 8 retired. Both Bill Dickey and Yogi Berra wore it while calling pitches for the Yankees and leading their teams into numerous World Series. Why Berra ever got to wear the number in the first place is surprising. Dickey's number should have been retired a long time before both players had it retired in 1972. Did any two catchers on the same team have more success than these two Yankees?

Dickey, who played with Ruth, Gehrig, and DiMaggio, helped the Yankees win eight American League pennants and seven World Series titles. I admire everything I have read or heard about the quiet, unassuming strength of the man known as Arkansas Bill. He hit for average (career

.313, second highest for a catcher), knocked 202 home runs, had a strong arm, and handled pitchers as well as anyone. He lived in Kensett, Arkansas, during his teen years. Kensett is about a mile from where I used to have an office when I preached for the Cloverdale Church of Christ in Searcy. While living there, I heard that he died in Lonoke, a town about 45 miles away. If I had known that I lived so closely to him, I would have tried to visit him.

Berra's October success was better than Dickey's or anyone else in baseball history. During his 17-year career, the Yankees appeared in the Series 14 times, winning ten. Berra holds six World Series records, and trails only Mantle and Ruth on six other lists.

Yogi was a tremendous athlete. He surprised everyone. Many called him an ape because of his size and appearance. He responded by saying, "I don't hit with my face." He needed Dickey to "learn him everything I know" about catching. That took some work, but hitting came easily for Berra. He had 358 home runs to go along with a .285 lifetime batting average. He is a funny man, filled with all kinds of wit and wisdom. Most people know at least one of his famous statements, although he claims, "I really didn't say everything I said."

I like Yogi because he, like Whitey Ford, was an overachiever. He was a winner, not because he had the best size and talent, but because he worked hard to excel. During his playing career, it was his attitude and work ethic, along with talent, that paved the way to his success. He was the catcher of my youth. He managed that 1964 team, then he got the shaft. It wasn't right. Even at age ten, I thought it wasn't right; I was sentimental loyalist, of course. And from what I have read in recent years, I now know it wasn't right. And George Steinbrenner wasn't even the boss then, but he too fired Yogi, in 1985.

There have been other great catchers that I have admired, like Elston Howard, Thurman Munson, and Jorge Posada. As a boy, I didn't know Elston Howard was the first African-American to play for New York. I never even thought about his skin color. I was just impressed with his batting and catching skills. I loved the way number 32 held the bat up high; it was a reflection of how he carried himself, both on and off the field.

Munson was tough. He was a competitor. He deserved to be named the first Yankee captain after Lou Gehrig. He was the league's most valuable player in 1976 and led the Yankees to three straight pennants in the 70s. I also liked Munson because he didn't like the Red Sox. He died too soon.

Posada was another tough competitor who overcame many obstacles to become a great catcher, and he never wore batting gloves. Because of Mantle, I like all switch-hitters. I especially liked watching him pull the ball with power from the left side of the plate. His swing reminded me of Roger Maris, a thing of beauty. He was part of the World Series winning Yankees five times.

THERE IS CRYING IN BASEBALL

"I cried many years' worth of tears that day."

—Joe Torre

DO GROWN MEN cry? Whether it was taught or just observed, I was sure the answer was no. My generation was clear on this: crying was for women, children, and weak men. Men, we were told, were supposed to be strong, tough, warriors who never let their emotional guards down. I have a sneaking suspicion, though, that even those who didn't cry wanted to several times in their lives. Since my early adult years, I have seen many men cry and, some have seen me cry. I never thought there was anything wrong with it. I still don't, and I am glad that recent generations have not been misguided about it.

In one of the classic moments of *A League of Their Own*, manager Jimmy Dugan (played by Tom Hanks) criticizes

– 57 –

his right fielder Evelyn Gardner (played by Bitty Schram), for throwing to the wrong base. "Now you start using your head," he says. He walks back into the dugout and she begins to cry. "Are you crying?" he asks.

"No."

"Are you crying?" Raising his voice he asks again, "Are you crying? There's no crying. There's no crying in baseball."

A great line from a great movie. But the guy was wrong.

Joe Torre wrote *Chasing the Dream* after the Yankees won the World Series in his inaugural season as the Yankees skipper. When he was hired after the 1995 season, one New York paper called him "Clueless Joe." The press can be brutal, and very wrong at times. In his autobiography, Torre described his dream which began in his teens and continued throughout his playing and managing career. At age 17, he watched game four of the 1957 World Series in Milwaukee, a game in which his brother Frank hit a home run. The Braves won that game and the World Series. "That's when the World Series became my dream. I fell asleep that night dreaming about it."

Torre's dream, like mine, continued for about 40 years, and he too wondered if it would ever come true, but it finally did. "Thirty-six years and 4,272 games since I put on a major league uniform for the first time, my dream had come true." And he cried. "I cried many years' worth of tears that day in Baltimore [when we won the pennant]."

And why not? There *is* crying in baseball, and his dream of going to the World Series had finally come true.

On the day my dream came true and just before the playing of the national anthem, I called my daughter Lori. It was just a few minutes past noon in Arkansas, and I knew it was close to the time when she would be home for lunch. I was disappointed to hear the answering machine, but I left a message, something like, "Where are you? Listen to this and you will know where I am." I held the phone away from me, so she could hear the song. The crowd noise escalated after "and the home of the brave," then I heard, "Daddy?" It was my little girl, all grown up and married now. "Daddy, it's me."

I have always been touched by the playing of "The Star Spangled Banner." When I played high school hockey, I often got a lump in my throat when I stood on the blue line during the song, and I still find it easy to get teary eyed every time I stand for the song before a game. Being at Yankee Stadium was no exception. At the other end of the phone was the familiar voice of a young lady who loves baseball—her favorite team is the Braves—and is married to a fine young man named Jonathan who also loves the game, but he's an Astros fan. She asked, "Daddy, did you cry when you got to the Stadium?" "No," I told her, choking on my words, "but I am now."

Lori told me how happy she was that I was living my dream and that she hoped she didn't have to wait until she was 51 to fulfill her dream of watching a Braves game in Atlanta. I told her I really doubted that she would have to wait that long. I couldn't say any more than that because I knew that Jonathan already had tickets for a game in Atlanta on July 30, their first anniversary.

Lori asked a good question. I was a little surprised that I hadn't cried when I first eyed the Stadium or at any time prior to the playing of the national anthem. There was so much excitement and many things to do, like seeing the field, walking around the Stadium, visiting the monuments, and getting settled into my seat. I guess I didn't have time to get sentimental and cry. It would have been okay, though, because there is crying in baseball.

As the game went on, I was able to speak with both of my sons. My older son Joshua was always the most excitable among our children, and he was ecstatic that I was at the game. He had called me one afternoon from Wrigley Field, and another time, he called while on his way to Atlanta to watch the Braves. We watched a game together at Coors Field. All of these were special sharing times for us. When Daniel called me on a break from work, he wanted to hear about my exciting day at the Stadium. Several years earlier, I had correctly answered a trivia question from a Lubbock radio station; the prize was two tickets to a Rangers game in Arlington. That game and the drive home the next day were very special for the two of us.

I wish I could have spoken with Bev during the Yankees game, but I had our only cell phone, and while she was at work, she was not able to make a call. My mind was full of family memories of the many times the five of us went to the youth sports complex in Searcy, Arkansas, for baseball and softball games. How I wished all of us could have been together for this game. Even though I would have been the only one cheering for the Yankees, I still would have enjoyed the presence of each of them.

The Braves are the favorite team of
the author's children Lori,
Josh, and Daniel. In 2012, the
three were at Turner Field
to watch Chipper Jones play his final game in Atlanta.

For the game that day, no one threw out the first pitch, a tradition I thought took place at every game. If only I would have known, I would have been quick to volunteer. What a thrill that would have been: to stand on the field with 48,000 fans watching me toss the ball to the Yankee catcher before the game began. I was okay with not getting the call; I had had plenty of thrills already.

Newcomer Carl Pavano was the Yankees starting pitcher. He fired one pitch and his no-hit bid was over, but he got out of the inning by striking out the next three batters. When the Yankees came to bat, Gary Sheffield blasted a home run with Bernie Williams, who had singled, on base. Just like that the Yanks were leading 2-0. I felt certain that this was going to be a day that I would see many Yankees cross the plate. Even though the Rays won the game, it was still a great day. It was my special day. So many wonderful things—all greater than a dream—were happening.

An interesting event took place in about the fourth or fifth inning. Four young men (probably in their early twenties), looking to improve their seats, asked if anyone was sitting in the seats just down from me. "Not yet," I smiled, then moved to let them pass. We spoke to each other a few times, and I was glad they were there, until I looked over at them in about the sixth inning. Three of them were asleep. Asleep? During a game at Yankee Stadium? I was appalled. It was embarrassing; I wanted to wake them up and demand that they leave immediately. I was sure that I would never do something as despicable as sleeping during a game at Yankee Stadium.

After the Rays batted in their half of the seventh, it was time to stand and sing. Jack Norworth wrote the words to "Take me Out to the Ball Game" in 1908 (it was revised in 1927). It has become a great tradition, sung at nearly every game in every ballpark in the middle of the seventh inning. I love it. It brings a smile to a person's face, and sometimes, a tear to the eye. People should be happy at a baseball game. I certainly was. (I have always wondered, however, why fans sing the song when they are already *at* the ball game.)

Sometimes baseball fans can't avoid recalling unhappy moments. When baseball resumed after the September 11 attacks, "God Bless America" was added to ball park activities. At Yankee Stadium, the tradition continues. It is the only venue that invites fans to sing both songs during the seventh inning stretch of every game. It is enough to make a person, who wasn't already crying, cry.

A light rain began to fall in the eighth inning, replaced by a mild downpour in the ninth. Nothing dampened my spirits that day, except when the game was over, and I had to leave. The game was over in less than three hours. I wasn't ready to leave, but the security people were asking me to leave. I had to go.

I took my time exiting the stands, picking up drink cups, and gazing one last time at the field. I hastened to the Yankees store before leaving and worked my way through the crowd to buy a few souvenirs. Closing time approached, and there was another push to get people out and to leave the Stadium. Before returning to the subway I hurried to a few shops and bought more souvenirs. I was surprised that even those shops were sending customers away. The only businesses staying open were the bars and restaurants.

I did an about-face to gaze one more time on the greatest sports venue in America, then caught the B train back to Manhattan. From there I worked my way back to the train station below Madison Square Garden, which took me to Penn Station in Newark. I had to switch trains on my way back to Bridgewater. I had just gotten seated on the final leg of the trip back when my phone rang. I answered and heard, "Hi Ron, this is Bobby Murcer." Just one more magnificent part of a terrific day!

Bobby Murcer joined the Yankees in the 60s and was touted as the next Mickey Mantle, the one who would continue the tradition following Ruth, DiMaggio, and Mantle of great Yankee outfielders. He instantly became my second favorite Yankee. After a few years, he and Thurman Munson became two of the best players and fan favorites. They were touted as the next M & M boys. I liked Murcer's attitude, his hustle, and his Oklahoma accent. I tried to stand in the batter's box and swing the bat the way he did (years before I had stopped trying to hit like Mantle; I just couldn't do it) which I eventually mastered and utilized all the years I played softball.

Murcer was employed as a Yankees announcer at the time, and he was one of the most beloved by his listeners. I had a student whose wife's family attended the same church in Oklahoma as the Murcers. After calling the student's mother-in-law, I was given the Murcer's home number and called to see if there was any chance that I might be able to meet Bobby while I was in New York. It turned out he was in California on a scouting trip and hadn't checked his voice mail for several days. He apologized for not getting in touch with me sooner. He apologized to me? Yes, he was always a very kind man, undeniably a class act.

I talk baseball often with my friend and colleague Brad Pruitt. His favorite team is the Texas Rangers, in spite of the fact that he lived in New York for a few years of his early childhood. His dad, an electrician, got a job helping with the wiring of a new construction project, the World Trade Center buildings. While living in Manhattan, they attended church with the Murcers, and Brad's family received many tickets for Yankee games from Bobby.

During our conversation, I told him that I was a 51-year-old man, and I felt like a little kid. He said, "That's the way it is with most of us." Baseball will do that to you. It will keep a man young, and occasionally it will bring tears to his eyes. Murcer, at age 59, still had a childlike love for baseball. I do too.

Bobby Murcer was a tremendous Yankee. My dream and his dream were the same: to be a Yankee. About 18 months after learning he had brain cancer, his autobiography *A Yankee for Life* was published (May 2008). I wasted no time reading the book and wrote him an e-mail, but I didn't get a reply this time. Just a few weeks later, on July 12, he passed away. It was the same day that we had buried my dad in Colorado.

I returned to Bridgewater in time for the midweek Bible study. Adam introduced me as one of his former teachers "who is a huge Yankees fan," adding that I had just come from the Stadium. I remember a lady who spoke to me that evening. She said she and her husband moved to New Jersey more than 30 years ago, and she has always been a Yankees fan. She had watched on TV the game I had attended and asked me about a few things that happened. She told me that Bobby Murcer had been her favorite player since they moved to the northeast, so I told her I had spoken with him. I could tell she was a bit envious (in a good way, of course).

Yes! I went to Yankee Stadium. I felt a sense of accomplishment. My dream came true.

There have been other times when baseball has caused me to cry, or maybe it is more accurate to say baseball has broken my heart because I really do have difficulty producing tears. As a boy, I just couldn't understand how it could rain on a summer day when we had a game scheduled. Once I begged our coach to let us play after the rain had stopped and ruined the infield. We didn't play that day, and an eleven-year old boy cried a little and pouted a lot on the way home.

I remember seeing a picture of Mantle, sliding into a base. The caption stated that he injured himself on the play and would be out for several weeks. I was heartbroken. I don't think I shed a tear, but that news hurt me profoundly. I wasn't sure how I would survive as I waited for him to start playing again.

When CBS owned the Yankees in the 60s, most of their weekend home games were televised. I watched so many of those games. Mantle was still playing. He was in his final years, but he could still knock the ball into the seats. There wasn't much else to watch on our only television, an old black-and-white set, so I usually got to see those games. Occasionally, however, one of my siblings, probably Carol who despised the Yankees, would get to watch something else. It always saddened me when I missed one of those games.

Another crushing moment in my life was a game I played in the summer before my sophomore year in high school. I was playing right field. With the bases loaded and my team trailing by six or seven runs, the ball came to me. I charged it but it went right through my legs. By the time I retrieved the ball and threw it to the infielders, everyone had scored, and the game was over because of the ten-run rule. I sulked as I walked off the field with my head down.

My coach yelled. "Bontrager, get in here." I thought he would chew me out, but he didn't. He wanted me to run off the field with pride, showing that I wasn't a loser, even though I lost that chance, and we lost the game.

After the game, my last, I lingered on my way home. I had gotten a ride to the game, believing someone in my family would be there later to take me home, but the message didn't get to the right person. So I walked, too embarrassed to ask for a ride after my game-ending error. I began the six-mile trek home, thinking about baseball, my mistakes, and my dreams. I realized I would never play for the Yankees, so I decided to call it quits for the summer. A few days later, I went to Iowa and worked and played on the farms with my cousins for the next five weeks. I wish now I wouldn't have quit playing baseball, even though I got to enjoy Iowa. Iowa is a good place. There is a beautiful baseball field there—where corn used to grow.

I am still saddened when I think about that day, and it has torn me up when I have seen a boy or girl (a few times, my own children) do something similar. I have tried to be the first one to encourage the kids, to make sure they keep things in perspective and remember there will be other days to play ball.

Sometimes, baseball will make a person cry, and that's a good thing—even for a man.

Yankee Stadium, June 22, 2005

	1	2	3	4	5	6	7	8	9	R	H	E
Tampa Bay	0	0	0							0	1	0
Yankees	2	0	0							2	2	1

Tampa Bay's leadoff batter in the third reached on an infield error, but after a fly out to right, a double play ended the Rays' inning.

In New York's half of the third, 21-year old Scott Kazmir, who was drafted by the Mets and traded to the Rays in 2004, showed the poise of an established veteran and wasn't intimidated by his surroundings despite having given up that first inning home run. He had little difficulty in dealing with the Bombers in another three-up-and-three-down inning.

My Favorite Yankee First Basemen

Mention the Yankees and those who have played first base, and one name always comes to mind: Gehrig. Enough said. No argument here. He won the hearts of baseball fans. If it weren't for Babe Ruth, Lou Gehrig would be praised as the greatest Yankee ever. He was a lifetime .340 hitter. He had 493 home runs. He won the triple crown in 1934. He helped the Yankees win six World Series. Oh, and by the way, he played in 2,130 consecutive games.

People spoke of his power on the field and his quietness off it. Like Thurman Munson, he died too soon. But as the case often is, sorrow doesn't have the final word in death. Gehrig's dignity in his final years, added to his outstanding character and baseball career, resulted in his name being forever linked to the disease that took his life. Few know what Amyotrophic Lateral Sclerosis is, but many know about Lou Gehrig Disease.

Two great baseball trivia questions are asked related to Gehrig's consecutive games streak. The first: who did Lou Gehrig replace as first baseman of the Yankees to begin the streak (actually the streak began one game before he became the regular first baseman, when he entered the game as a pinch hitter)? The second: who replaced Gehrig on the day the streak ended?

Neither Wally Pipp nor Babe Dahlgren (answers to the above questions) is among my favorite New York first basemen, but Joe Pepitone, Don Mattingly, and Tino Martinez are. So was Mantle, of course, definitely my favorite in every category that involved him; he played first base his final two years. Pepitone was the flamboyant "city slicker" that any boy of ten could learn to love. He was the up-and-coming first baseman of my youth. As it turned out, though, he was a disappointment. He probably wasted more talent than the time it takes Bill Gates to count his money.

Mattingly, however, was different. "Donnie Baseball" had all kinds of talent and utilized it fully, achieving much success in spite of an ailing back that led to an early retirement. Even with limited playing time and a short career, he deserves to be in Cooperstown.

The thing I liked about Tino Martinez was his swing. He had power to spare and showed it often during his years with the Yankees. He played on five World Series teams from 1996 to 2001. I hated to see him go after the 2001 season, and was glad to see him don the pinstripes again in 2005.

ALWAYS A YANKEE

*"I'd like to thank the good Lord
for making me a Yankee."*

—Joe DiMaggio

I DON'T KNOW exactly when I became a Yankees fan, but I don't ever remember not being one. At some point in my life, the Yankees and Mickey Mantle became my favorites. Nothing has ever happened to change that, either. Mantle was the favorite player of his era, and his popularity increased after his retirement.

Perhaps I began to like the Yankees because my older brother Warren played one summer on a Little League team called the Yankees. That was when we lived in Iowa. We moved to Colorado when I was six. If memory serves me correctly, the team uniforms had pinstripes. The only problem about that team is that the pinstripes were red, maybe even pink, but definitely not blue. Maybe I'm wrong about the color, but I do remember the team's name. I cheered for the Yankees then because my brother, always one of my heroes (except during his early teens when he would beat me up if I looked at him the wrong way), played for the Yankees. Maybe that is how my fascination began.

Maybe I started liking the New York Yankees because of the influence of my best friend, Casey Elliott, whose father played a few seasons in the minors. The Elliotts lived in a big house on a hillside across the street from our place on the west side of Colorado Springs. Casey and I were inseparable while in elementary school, especially during the summers when we played and talked baseball. We watched "ABC's Wide World of Sports" and then hurried outside to mimic those games in my backyard, or at the school playground. We made up our own teams and played games against the pros. We played all sports, but our favorite was baseball, and the New York Yankees was our team. CBS, the owners of the Yankees, aired weekend games at the Stadium. We listened to Dizzy Dean and Pee Wee Reese call the games and when the M & M boys came up, he was Roger Maris, and I was Mickey Mantle.

Chester Romero, another boyhood friend, recently reminded me that we were Yankees fans for as long as he can remember. The two of us and many others often gathered on the playground at Whittier Elementary for games of softball and baseball, even though the sign on the back-stop said, "no baseballs allowed." In my first year of organized baseball, Chester played shortstop, and I played third base. The next year I moved to second. We played together on many other teams. Often, I would pedal to his house, and he would ride on the back of my bike on our way to practice. His favorite player then was Bobby Richardson; he remembers that mine was Mickey Mantle.

Another possibility of my becoming a Yankees fan is that I found it easy to follow a winner. The other favorite teams during my youth were the Bill Russell-led Celtics, John Wooden's UCLA Bruins, and the Green Bay Packers. They won many championships, but no team had more success than the Yankees. Just in my lifetime, the Bronx Bombers have won eleven championships. Not many fans can say their teams have won that many in their entire history, and the Yankees were the champions of baseball sixteen times before I was born.

My earliest memories of cheering for the Yankees go back to 1963. My dad sold Chevrolets, so we were members of the local Corvair club. Every month there was a club activity on a Sunday. On October 6, we were at a picnic area in the mountains when I heard that someone had turned on a radio. It was game four of the World Series. Mantle hit a home run off Sandy Koufax to tie the game in the seventh, but Los Angeles regained the lead on an unearned run in the same inning and went on to win the game, 2-1, for a four-game sweep. My sister Carol went home happy. I didn't. At the time, the Yankees had won 20 World Series titles and lost eight; this was the only time they had been swept.

I don't remember any other Yankees game before 1964. Everything came together for me that year. Oh how I remember 1964! It was a turning point in my life, and not because the Beatles had invaded America that February, although my hair length did begin to change soon after that. All through the season I devoured the sports pages, pored over stats, and defended my team. Yankees baseball must have been deeply ingrained in my mind because I never doubted that I would see my team playing again in October. I have never forgotten the eight position players who started most of the games that year, along with the reserves, pitchers, and coaches.

Unfortunately Game 7 of the Series ended on a sad note. So many times I have relived that final out. Usually the ball drops, the ninth inning rally continues, and Mantle hits a game-winning home run. My friend Tom Martin, a huge Cardinals fan, gave me David Halberstam's *October 1964* with this note: "Just remember which team wins in '64." I always have and always will remember, no matter how hard I try to forget. I have been waiting ever since for an October rematch. I thought it would happen for sure in 2004, and the Yankees would end my 40 years of grieving. But a 3-0 lead in the American League Championship Series wasn't enough, and the Red Sox won four straight games, and then they won four more against the Cardinals to end the 85-year "curse of the Bambino."

During that 1964 campaign, management had lost confidence in Yogi Berra in his initial season as field manager. He was fired after the Game 7 loss, but I recall spending the winter visualizing how the Yanks would be playing again in October. No one was more optimistic than I. I was a Yankees fan, after all, and I couldn't wait for winter to pass and spring to arrive. Up to that point in my life the Yankees and October baseball went together about as often as Columbus Day and October.

My optimism didn't help in 1965, the team's first losing season in forty years, or in 1966 when the Yankees finished in the cellar for the first time since 1912, or any other season until the magical American bicentennial year of 1976. I never stopped being a Yankees fan in those years. I continued to check the sports section nearly every day for scores, stats, standings, and that day's starting pitchers.

When Mantle announced his retirement before the 1969 season, my loyalty to the team didn't fade, even though my "career" as a baseball player would also end that summer. During high school and early college years, I worked part-time as a sports writer for *The Gazette*. During three summers, I was also the announcer and official scorer at the city's best baseball field, where I watched hundreds of American Legion and semi-pro games. I was surrounded by baseball players and information. Those were fantastic jobs.

The Yankees didn't win any pennants during those years, but I still cheered for them and followed them closely. When George Steinbrenner headed up a group of 14 who purchased the team from CBS for a mere ten million dollars in 1973, I remained a fan, but I was not happy with some of the things that were done in those early years. Steinbrenner announced "absentee ownership," a promise that did not last long.

I didn't mind his constant micromanaging of the team, and I didn't care that he spent a lot of money and made many enemies as he tried to assemble the best team in the majors. What bothered me was the way he treated his managers: hiring and firing them like a train on a subway, moving rapidly down the tracks only to stop and start all over again. In the summer of 1977, I wrote a letter to the editors of *Sports Illustrated* in response to a critical article about Steinbrenner's handling of the team. I wanted to add my disgust with the way he was running things. I thought it was a good letter, but it wasn't published.

As time went on, I realized he was just trying to win championships. I like that. To all those who criticize the Yankees as "the best team money can buy" with "the highest payroll in baseball," I usually ask, "Don't you wish the owner of your favorite team would do what it takes to have a team that is always near the top?" If I had ever met "The Boss," I would have thanked him for doing so much to help the Yankees win.

Hiring Joe Torre was one of the best things Steinbrenner ever did. There were 20 managerial changes (Billy Martin led the way, being hired and fired five times) and just two championships from 1973–1991. Buck Showalter managed the team for the next four seasons, which at the time was the longest tenure in the Steinbrenner era. Showalter brought the Yankees from mediocrity to contenders again. Torre led the Yankees to four championships in his first five years. His dream of going to the World Series came true in his first season as skipper of the Yanks. "Maybe the good Lord was just waiting for me to put on the pinstripes," Torre quipped. After 17 seasons and no final game victory in October, Yankees fans were again doing what Yankees know best, cheering for their world champions. The party began at the Stadium when Charlie Hayes squeezed the ball for the final out in the Game 6 victory on October 26, 1996. Three days later, an estimated 3 million fans cheered the Yankees as they paraded through the Canyon of Heroes in Manhattan.

I married a wonderful lady who is quite an athlete (no telling how good she would have been if she had grown up after Title IX went into effect), but she is not a Yankees fan.

We lived in Brazil in the mid-80s (before the internet), and it was difficult to get baseball news there. Still, it seemed like every October something inside me would just go off automatically, urging me to get the bat, balls, and gloves to remind my children not only of the great American pastime but also of the most successful team in baseball history.

Maybe I was destined to be a Yankees fan because my family history indicates that significant events and Yankees championships go together.

My dad Amos Bontrager was born in 1918. The Yankees didn't have a winning record that season (just 60-63), which was not unusual during the mediocre pre-Ruth years, but America won the War that November, and that was a good thing. The Red Sox had won the Fall Classic just weeks before (but they never won again in the twentieth-century). Americans had been inspired by George M. Cohan's "Over There," a new patriotic song that inspired confidence that the war would soon end because "The Yanks are coming." My mom, Margaret Rhodes, was born in 1927. What a year that was! The Yankees won 110 games and swept the Series, the Babe hit 60 home runs, the term "Murderer's Row" was born, and the Yankees dynasty was established. My parents married in the fall of 1947. The Yankees won the Series that year.

My sister Judy was born in 1949, which was the first of five consecutive Yankee championships under new manager Casey Stengel. Warren came along two years later, and the Yankees had their third straight title in Mantle's rookie season. Then Carol, the Yankees-hater, was born in 1952, just days after New York beat her Dodgers for championship number 15. Patty was born in 1956, and the Yankees won again, thanks in part to Don Larsen's perfect game. The victory was special as the Yankees got revenge on the Dodgers who had beaten them the year before.

New York won ten American League pennants during Stengel's 12 years as manager and won the Series seven times. I was born in 1954, the year the Yankees won 103 games (the most ever by a Stengel-managed team), but New York didn't even win the pennant. The Yankees welcomed me with an outstanding season, but the Indians proved to be better that year.

Bev and I married in 1978—another banner year for the Yankees, a second-straight Dodgers-whipping. Especially sweet was seeing Goose Gossage on the mound for the final out in the one-game playoff with Boston, the League Championship Series against the Royals, and the championship-clinching Game 6 of the Series.

There were no championships in the years our children were born, although there was great joy with the birth of our first son Joshua in 1981. The Yankees went to the Series that October, but they lost to the Dodgers, who came back from a 0-2 deficit to win it in six games. A few days later I received a postcard from Carol with just four words: "How 'bout those Dodgers!" Ouch. But I was ok with the loss. After all, the previous August I became Daddy to a very special little guy.

Something inside me was whispering that the Yankees would win in the year of my first grandchild. Early in 2008 Abigail Towell and Aidan Bontrager were born, but championship Number 27 had to wait, but not for long. The next year I celebrated their first birthdays and a Yankees championship.

Growing up in Colorado, far removed from "Dixie," I don't remember people disliking the Bronx Bombers for any reason other than the fact that their favorite team—no matter who it was—kept losing to the Yankees. Living in the South since 1988, I have discovered there is another reason to dislike them (hate is a better word but seems insufficient at times). It is the name. Southerners just don't like the word yankee. The Civil War ended 150 years ago, but yankees are still despised by some in the South. On miserable days in Arkansas, my friend Leland Hyde would usually ask, "Ron, what do you think of this yankee weather?" He was cussing, I know he was.

We moved to Searcy in 1988 and lived there for nine years. Our children began cheering for Atlanta, and they had a lot to cheer about. The Braves began an incredible run of division championships in 1991 and won the Series in

1995. I became a Braves fan too, but I always told the kids that the Braves were only my second favorite team.

While we were in Arkansas, the Yankees were never higher than fourth place until 1993. They finished second that year and had the best record in the American League in '94 when the strike ended the season prematurely. An October came and went, and there was no World Series. Those were dark, scary days, Halloweenish days throughout that October. It was tragic and disheartening. It was worse than any year we lived in Brazil when we heard very little baseball news (and that came late, usually in a letter from a friend who knew I was a baseball fan), and we couldn't even watch the Series. At least the games were *played*. Baseball fans will always brood about that dreadful 1994 season as a disappointing time in American history. It was not as bad as the stock market crash of 1929 or the bombing of Pearl Harbor in 1941, but it was still disappointing.

Then came 1995, and the Yankees made the playoffs as the wild card team, their first postseason appearance since 1981. New York beat Seattle in their first two games at home, but lost three straight in the Emerald City. I thought the Yankees had it won in Game 5 when Randy Velarde (who helped my alma mater Lubbock Christian University win the NAIA World Series in 1983) drove in the go-ahead run in the eleventh, but the Mariners came back with two

– 83 –

runs in the bottom of the inning to eliminate my team. Even after the loss, they were still my team.

When October 1996 arrived, more and more people found out I liked the Yankees. It seemed that the more people who heard I was Yankees fan, the more I heard disgusting comments about the Yankees and their fans. "Them's fightin' words" is what I heard from many rednecks. I soon found out that neither a yankee nor a Yankees fan is welcome in the South.

When the Series was set that year, the Braves against the Yankees, and I heard that Fox would be airing the games, I made an important discovery. Up to that time I didn't think our TV could get the local Fox station. I was ready to invest in cable, whatever it cost, to be able to watch the Yankees play in October. Turned out that all we needed was a different connection between the antenna and TV; it was free, just like that 1964 Series. I watched every game with delight—even the two Braves' wins in New York—because memories of childhood and Yankees postseason games were back in my mind.

The Yankees beat the Braves on a Saturday night to end the series in six games. I was the only one rejoicing in our house that night. I repressed bringing it up the next day at church, but after the song leader mentioned it, I was compelled to express my pleasure about the Series. I don't know if anyone assembled that morning shared my joy because nearly all were either Atlanta or St. Louis fans.

After we moved to Lubbock, Texas, in 1997, New York earned a spot in the playoffs every year through 2007. And I got the same kind of treatment from many Texans when they discovered that I cheered for the Yankees.

Sometimes I'll ask, "Why do you hate the Yankees?" The answer is usually something like, "Because they buy their championships," or "they have too many titles already and it's time for someone else to win." The first comment seems legitimate, but in reality money has not been enough to win pennants, not for the Yankees or any of the other big-spending teams. To the second statement, a simple question usually identifies its fallacy. When I ask, "If the Dallas Cowboys go to the Super Bowl the next ten years and win seven of them, would you think it is time for someone else to win it," the answer has never been "yes." What a difference it is when your favorite team wins. I should know because mine does it often.

I know it's just a southern thing to hate that word. I am convinced there would be more New York fans in the South if the team were still called the Highlanders. That name doesn't sound offensive, but the words yankees and Yankees do not go over well.

In the big picture, however, isn't it a word that instills pride for Americans, who are known worldwide as yankees? Songs like "I'm a Yankee Doodle Dandy" and "Over There" make us feel good about being Americans, especially around July 4th which is right in the middle of the baseball season. Yankee is good enough for me, but not for many southerners. I had a teacher who did mission work in South Africa. Upon moving there, he was called a yankee and didn't like it. He was told that white men in South Africa were called British or yankee. He said, "call me British."

Another pleasant boyhood memory of being a Yankees fan is hearing Dizzy Dean and Pee Wee Reese on CBS weekend broadcasts of games at Yankee Stadium. They were as much a part of my early years as Mel Allen and Red Barber were to radio listeners a generation before me. Allen was "the Voice of the Yankees," broadcasting games from 1939–1964. Barber was in the booth the next 13 years. Dean had so many classic phrases: a line drive was "a blue darter"; after a home run he would say, "that ball was tagged"; and perhaps his most famous phrase was, "he slud into third." Occasionally he would sing "The Wabash Cannonball." I was ten or eleven when I wrote him a letter. A short time later I got a reply that began, "Sure was good hearin' from you, podner." Dizzy Dean was down home country, from Arkansas. He was a Southerner, one of only a few, who would say good things about my favorite baseball team, the New York Yankees.

That letter I received from Dizzy Dean is framed and hangs on a wall in my baseball "museum." My museum is nothing fancy, and there is no admission fee, but there is a lot of baseball history there—mostly about the Yankees, of course. I have three hat racks, each one holds the hats of ten Major League teams. There is an autographed Mantle picture (another gift from my Cardinals friend Tom, a going-away present when we left Arkansas), a picture of Ruth and Gehrig in a large frame (a gift from Joshua), and all of my baseball books, which now number over one hundred and are placed on bookcases that I made. Some of the books are from my youth, but most were purchased or given to me in recent years. My room also displays a program from an early 1951 Yankees game at Fenway Park, which lists Mantle's uniform as Number 6. It's where I keep all my baseball cards, except a 1969 Mantle card that is in a safe deposit box at a bank, including every card in the 2004 Yankees Classics set by Upper Deck. In addition, there are many small keepsakes from my youth, souvenirs from my trips to New York, and my ever-increasing cups from MLB teams.

The baseball room was Bev's idea. When we moved into our house in 1998, the kitchen was large enough, and we didn't have any formal dining furniture anyway, so she suggested that the dining room be my office, and that we could turn it into a baseball room. Am I blessed with a wonderful wife or what? It was also her idea to put a baseball border around the room when we wallpapered it with a vertical lines design, which was the closest thing to pin stripes we could find. We moved again in the summer of 2014; now the new house has a baseball room.

Greg Hall wrote the following poem which was featured on *ESPN Radio* during the 2000 season. It does a superb job of summing up what baseball and what being a Yankees fan mean to me.

>Baseball is grass, chalk, and dirt displayed the same
>   yet differently
>In every park that has ever heard the words play
>   ball.
>Baseball is a passion that bonds and divides all
>   those who know it.
>Baseball is a pair of hands stained with newsprint,
>A set of eyes squinting to read a box score,
>A brow creased in an attempt to recreate a three-
>   hour game
>From an inch square block of type.
>Baseball is the hat I wear to mow the lawn.
>Baseball is a simple game of catch
>and the never-ending search for the perfect
>   knuckleball.

Baseball is Willie vs. Mickey, Gibson vs. Koufax,
and Buddy Biancalana vs. the odds.
Baseball links Kansan and Missourian, American
and Japanese,
But most of all father and son.
Baseball is the scent of spring,
The unmistakable sound of a double down the line,
And the face of a 10-year-old emerging from the
pile of bodies
With a worthless yet priceless foul ball.
Baseball is a language of very simple words that
tell unbelievable magic tales.
Baseball is three brothers in the same uniform on
the same team for one brief summer
Captured forever in a black and white photo on a
table by the couch.
Baseball is a glove on a shelf, oiled and tightly
wrapped,
Slumbering through the stark winter months.
Baseball is a breast pocket bulging with a transis-
tor radio.
Baseball is the reason there are transistor radios.
Baseball is a voice in a box describing men you've
never met,
In a place you've never been,

Doing things you'll never have the chance to do.
Baseball is a dream that you never really give up
    on.
Baseball is precious.
Baseball is timeless.
Baseball is forever.

I have always been a fan of the New York Yankees, the greatest team in baseball. Baseball is everything Hall described, and more. And less, too. That line near the end, "in a place you've never been" no longer applies to me because the dream of this Yankees fan has come true.

Yankee Stadium, June 22, 2005

	1	2	3	4	5	6	7	8	9	R	H	E
Tampa Bay	0	0	0	2						2	4	0
Yankees	2	0	0	0						2	2	1

Pavano recorded his fifth strikeout when the first Rays batter came up in the fourth inning. One out later, it looked like he was cruising along, but Travis Lee and Jonny Gomes changed things in a hurry. Lee singled up the middle, and Gomes blasted a game-tying home run into left field seats. With the score tied 2-2, Aubrey Huff singled but was gunned down trying to steal second, by John Flaherty, which ended the inning.

The Yankees went down quietly in their half of the fourth. It was another quick inning for Kazmir, who got Hideki Matsui, the eleventh consecutive batter retired by the young lefty, to end the inning.

My Favorite Yankee Second Basemen

There have been two Yankees to play second base that quickly won my affection. As a boy it was Bobby Richardson. In early adult years, it was Willie Randolph.

Richardson had the right perspective about life and played second about as well as any of his contemporaries. He is the only player to be named World Series MVP from a losing team. This happened in 1960 when he batted .367 with 12 runs batted in against Pittsburg. He did even better against the Cardinals in 1964, batting .406. Richardson retired when he could have continued for many more years, but he loved the Lord and his family, and he wanted others to know about it. His beliefs and lifestyle were obvious in an arena where Christianity was often off-limits. I enjoyed reading the chapter about him in Bill Madden's *Pride of October* and his autobiography. Mickey Mantle was not known for living the way Richardson did, but the Mick had a deep respect for Richardson, so much so that

Mantle requested his former teammate to speak at his funeral service.

Randolph was also one of the best second baseman of his generation. His stats weren't good enough for Cooperstown, but he was a winner, a class act if there ever was one. He played his position well and had many key hits, helping the Yankees win three consecutive pennants from 1976 through 1978. He showed that a quiet man—his actions spoke loudly—could do his job well. I always thought there was something special about him—that he really *knew* baseball. I wasn't surprised when he joined Joe Torre's staff and was later hired to manage the other New York team. His firing in 2008 was a classless act by the Mets.

TEAM OCTOBER

*"Dominance and dynasties—
nobody comes close to the Yankees."*

—Yogi Berra

LINDY MCDANIEL PITCHED for five major league teams, including the Yankees from 1968–1973, in a career that spanned 21 seasons. When he was released by the Royals after the 1975 season, he was second on the all-time list for games pitched and innings pitched by a reliever. He told me, "When you put on the pinstripes, you're putting on history."

History indeed. Successful history. Unique history.

There is no other professional sports team in America with as many championships as the Yankees. The Montreal Canadiens of the National Hockey League have won the coveted Stanley Cup 24 times, but no other professional

— 95 —

team in any sport comes close to the success of the New York Yankees.

October, baseball, and the Yankees go together like "Tinkers to Evers to Chance." Like Moe, Curly, and Larry, it is difficult to think of one without thinking of the others. They go together like Shoeless Joe Jackson, Kevin Costner, and "If you build it, he will come." Except for a long dry spell for the Yankees from 1982 until 1994, the three are about as common as a young boy running to a sandlot with his bat, ball, and glove.

Remove the 1976–1981 seasons, and the absence of the Yankees from post-season play began after the 1964 Series loss to the Cardinals and continued until the 1995 Wild Card team lost to Seattle. That was thirty years and only five times making it to the second season. While many franchises would give anything to make the playoffs "only" five times in 30 years (between 1965 and 1994, there were only seven teams that played in October more than five times), the drought was very long for the greatest team in baseball.

To those familiar with Yankee teams from 1995 through 2012, when the team played every October but one, that long absence of Yankee baseball in October seems hard to believe. Those familiar with Yankee success in the years prior to 1965 find it even more incredulous. From 1921 until 1964, the Yankees were in the World Series 28 times. *Twenty-eight times!* An amazing sixty-four per cent of the time. And that was back in an era when only one team (that's right, *one*) from each league, not five as there are now, played in October. During that stretch of 44 seasons, the Yankees never went more than three years without winning a pennant, and for 18 seasons, from 1947 through 1964, they won every pennant except three. Considering all Yankees teams from 1921 until the end of the century, there were 26 World Series champion banners flying in the Bronx. During the 91 baseball seasons from 1921 through 2012, the Yankees played October baseball 50 times.

All that playing and winning in October didn't begin, though, until 1921, during the Babe's second of 15 seasons in pinstripes. And what a beginning was ushered in that year.

There had been very little success by the "other" New York team that began play in 1903 as one of eight teams in the newly established American League. Even though manager John McGraw of the New York Giants opposed the idea of another team in the great Metropolis, Ban Johnson, president of the new league, believed there had to be an American League team in New York for the new league to survive.

After the American League's first two seasons, the Orioles left Baltimore to take up residence in New York City. The new team in Gotham was originally called the Highlanders because home games were played in the

Washington Heights section of Manhattan's upper east-side, on Broadway between 165th and 168th streets, at Hilltop Park, which was the highest point on the island. The Highlanders played there from 1903–1912. New York's Columbia-Presbyterian Medical Center now occupies that real estate. In 1913 the Giants reluctantly allowed their American League nemesis to share the Polo Grounds with them.

McGraw and his star pitcher Christy Mathewson, who hurled three shutouts, led the Giants to an easy win in the inaugural World Series between National and American League teams in 1905. The Giants won four more pennants from 1911–1917, but lost the World Series each time, and four consecutive National League championships from 1921–24. The two wins in 1921 and 1922 were bittersweet for McGraw. Both victories were against the Yankees, who in 1913 took the name that symbolized America to the world, but McGraw's disgust continued. In 1920, Ruth's first year with the Yankees, and for the next two seasons, the Yankees drew more fans to the Polo Grounds than the Giants.

Yankee Stadium opened in 1923. It instantly became the greatest baseball park in America. The Coliseum in Rome and England's Wembley Stadium, which also opened in 1923, are the only two sports venues in the world that rival Yankee Stadium's size, significance, and history. It was built across the Hudson River in the Bronx, just a short distance from the Polo Grounds, and it would cast a long shadow over the Giants and their field. The Yankees won the Series in 1923, and the Giants would never again beat the Yankees in October, losing the next three times they met in New York and once more after the Giants relocated in San Francisco.

The Yankees played in the World Series for the first time in 1921. Prior to that year, there had been nineteen Octobers without Yankees baseball. Only seven of those years saw the Yankees win more games than they lost. An earthquake in baseball history was about to hit, one that a Richter scale could not go high enough to measure. It might be called a real "no-no" for the rest of the baseball world, especially by those adorable Red Sox fans.

The day was December 26, 1919. What a Christmas present for the Yankees! All Yankees. For the rest of time. Players and fans would enjoy "the gift that keeps on giving" for decades, even a century. For others, that day went down in history as the initial December "day of infamy." On that date, three names were forever etched into the baseball tapestry. One was a lady known only by her first name of Nanette. Another was Harry Frazee, the owner of the Boston Red Sox. The other—*the* other—was George Herman Ruth. The event that shaped baseball's future was Frazee's sale of the Babe to the Yankees.

What an interesting person Frazee was. Other words come to mind when thinking about Frazee, but my mom taught me, "If you don't have something good to say about a person, don't say anything at all." Frazee bought the Red Sox for a mere $500,000 in 1916. In the few years before "the date," the Red Sox were the best team in baseball. They had won the Series four times from 1912 to 1918. Ruth was emerging as baseball's most outstanding player when he was sold. How drastic of a move was this for the Red Sox? They went 85 years without winning another Series title. And the Yankees? They won 26 in the same time span.

The sale of Babe Ruth began what baseball people called "The Curse of the Bambino." So influential was the sale that New Englanders suffered through many seasons, including a few very close Series losses, and never thought another title would come to Boston.

Frazee sold Ruth for $100,000 and also received a $400,000 loan from the Yankees. He even risked losing Fenway Park, which he put up as collateral for the loan. He needed the money to finance *No, No Nanette,* a Broadway musical. You wonder why a guy like that ever got into baseball. Fortunately, he didn't stay long. In 1923, he sold the Red Sox, just four years after he sold baseball's greatest and most popular player. Baseball would never be the same. The Red Sox's fall and the Yankees rise began both immediately and simultaneously.

I feel sorry for Red Sox fans, especially those whom I know and whose friendship I highly value. But I don't feel bad for the Yankees. No, not at all. They just made the best of a bad situation. I mean, what else is a smart owner to do when Babe Ruth is on the market? As for Frazee: he went down in history, way down, as one of Boston's least-liked persons. He probably ranks high on the list with the likes of Bucky Dent and Aaron Boone.

My mom also said, "If you look down deep inside a person, you'll find something good." So it is with Mr. Frazee. He began something in 1918 that continues today. It is one of many wonderful baseball traditions that take place at every American professional baseball game as well as nearly all other American sports, professional and amateur. Many countries, in fact, do the same thing, following the precedent set by the United States. In Game 1 of the Series that year, Frazee, wanting to honor solders in Europe, brought in a band to play "The Star-Spangled Banner" during the seventh inning stretch. Players, servicemen, and other fans stood at attention and looked at the American flag and cheered wildly at the song's conclusion. Incidentally, Babe Ruth pitched the Red Sox to a 1-0 victory that afternoon. The song was played at the other World Series games that year. It became our national anthem in 1931, and the rest is history.

Babe Ruth changed the face of baseball. He led the American League in home runs with a mere 11 in 1918, but the next year, his last in Boston, he had 29 homers, the most in baseball's young history. When he walloped a staggering 54 in his first season with the Yankees, no other player hit more than 19, and only one team hit more home runs than he did. Many believe Ruth and his home run prowess contributed immensely to the return of baseball popularity after the 1919 Black Sox scandal had done so much to tarnish the national pastime.

Not everyone appreciated the changes. The Giants and manager McGraw did not like either the Yankees or Ruth and his home runs. Ty Cobb, baseball's best hitter in his day, also disliked the Babe for swinging for the fences, but word is that very few baseball people liked the Georgia Peach. Cobb and McGraw were old school baseball. To them, the game was about bunting for a base hit, putting the ball in the gap, getting hit by a pitch, or drawing a walk—anything possible to get to first. Then it was moving up the runner, one base at a time, and winning games by a run. Simple enough, right? That is certainly not the way most play baseball today.

Ruth hit home runs. Long home runs. Lots of home runs. Known by his numerous nicknames, among them the Sultan of Swat, the King of Swing, the Great Bambino, and the Tower of Power, George (as he was called by James Earl Jones's character in *Sandlot*) blasted 59 more home runs in his second year with the Yankees, and then he broke that record with a staggering 60 circuit clouts in 1927. McGraw was not impressed.

Yankee Stadium opened April 18, 1923. It was fitting that the first opponent was the Boston Red Sox, and that Ruth would hit a three-run home run to help the Yankees win the game, 4-1. It was also fitting that the Yankees would end the season winning their first World Series, beating their neighbors across the river, the New York Giants.

McGraw got one of his wishes that year: the Yankees were out of the Polo Grounds. He thought it was good-bye forever. Just a few years earlier, according to *The Yankee Encyclopedia*, he told Giants owner Charles Stoneham, "Chase the Yankees out of the Polo Grounds and make them build their own park in the Bronx, because once they go up there, they will be forgotten." Add that to the list of famous last words! The Yankees weren't going away. They weren't forgotten, either. They would hoist 26 pennants over their "park in the Bronx" the next 80 years. The Giants went on to win just two championships before moving west.

Boston finally won the World Series in 2004. It was the year to reverse the curse. Their fans coined the term, "Red Sox Nation." That phrase was everywhere it seemed, but the title was not the beginning of a dynasty as some boasted. I agree with the shirt I saw in a Manhattan store that stated, "Any idiot can win a title, but it takes a champion to be a dynasty." Interesting how a phrase like that only pops up after a team wins a championship. Meanwhile, back in the Bronx, the term Yankees Universe seems appropriate.

From 1936–1964, winning was the norm for the Yankees. It was expected. Whitey Ford said, "You kind of took it for granted around the Yankees that there was always going to be baseball in October." Comedian Joe E. Lewis stated, "Rooting for the Yankees is like rooting for U.S. Steel."

Joe DiMaggio was respected by all the Yankees, not just because of his talent, but also because of his efforts to overcome injury, sickness, and other setbacks. Few players ever worked as diligently as he did, just to play. And he played to win, which inspired teammates to do the same.

Yogi Berra commented on playing for the Yankees: "We just seemed to win every year. That's what made playing for the Yankees so much fun."

During the Stengel years the Yankees won ten pennants in 12 years. Every veteran expected to win the pennant and play in the World Series. Pay was not good when George Weiss was in charge of salaries; many players received nearly as much by being in the World Series as they received for the entire season. Hank Bauer, the tough Marine who played in the outfield for the Yankees from 1948–1959, chastised a young Mickey Mantle for not running out a ground ball by yelling, "Don't fool with my money," which was a reference to the regularity with which Bauer cashed Yankees World Series checks.

Every newcomer to the Yankees knew he had better play for the championship, or else he didn't belong. Nothing less than the pennant was acceptable.

There was a considerable amount of pride and honor playing for the Yankees. Berra said,

> Being part of the New York Yankees...feels like you're part of history. It's being connected to legends—Ruth, Gehrig, DiMaggio—and being part of a special family. Walking into Yankee Stadium for the first time, I felt like I was walking into something from the Bible.

He also said, "I'd rather be the Yankees' catcher than the President."

DiMaggio made the statement, "I want to thank the Good Lord for making me a Yankee." A sign bearing the quote hangs above the doorway that leads to the Yankees dugout; it is in plain sight for all Yankees who pass by it on their way to the playing field.

John Tullius remarked, "The magnitude of the Yankee achievement ultimately boggles even the fanatic's mind."

On being a Yankee, Marius Russo said, "I was very proud and lucky to be a Yankee, just being around and part of all those great guys."

On playing for the Yankees, Mickey Mantle said it is "the best thing that could ever happen to a ballplayer."

In more recent times, Derek Jeter commented on his being a Yankee: "To have the chance to play at Yankee Stadium and be on their team, I must be one of the lucky ones."

Jeter's teammate Paul O'Neill observed, "I hit the jackpot. I came here at the right time. I played with the right people. I was a little part of the right team. You expect to win but not the way we won."

Frank Devery and Frank Farrell were the original owners of the New York American League team that left Baltimore and began playing in The City in 1903. In 1915 they sold the team to Jacob Ruppert and Tillinghast L'Hommedieu Huston. Ruppert became the sole owner in 1922, and he and his heirs remained owners until 1945. Larry MacPhail, Dan Topping, and Del Webb bought the team and held it for nearly twenty years, selling it to the Columbia Broadcasting System in 1964 for $11.2 million. In 1973, CBS lost over one million dollars, selling the team to a group headed by George Steinbrenner. It is hard to imagine that a group could own the New York Yankees and lose money. The Boss turned things around quickly. His family now holds ownership of a franchise that in 2014 was worth $2.5 billion, the most of any professional sports team in America. I doubt that there will be a "For Sale" sign posted in front of the Stadium in my lifetime. The Boss once said, "Owning the Yankees is like owning the Mona Lisa. It's something that you'd never sell"

There was so much success for Yankee teams and their players that it is no wonder they have the largest fan base of any team in America. Most of my friends, who played baseball with me in the 60s, were Yankees fans, too. Goose Gossage has spoken about his upbringing in Colorado, far away from Yankee territory. His dad cheered for the Yankees, and so did he. My nephew Matt Bain used to work at a sporting goods store in Colorado Springs. When I saw him one day at work, I was amazed that there were so many Yankee things for sale at that store. He said they sold more Yankees memorabilia than any other team, including the one that plays their home games just 60 miles to the north.

As I walked around Manhattan and rode the subway, it dawned on me that there were Yankee hats, shirts, and jackets being worn by large numbers of people. When I rummaged through the stores, I noticed at least ten times more Yankee merchandise than any other team. Sure, there were a few Red Sox fans and a smattering of other teams' hats and shirts being worn. But I wondered if the Mets were still in New York. It was as if there were only one team in Metropolis, and it was the team with a long history of dominance and dynasties.

In 1929, the Yankees became the first team in major league baseball to sew numbers on the backs of their uniforms. The decision was made to help spectators identify the players. Numbers had previously been used in the minor leagues, by many college and pro football teams, and by the St. Louis Cardinals, who put small numbers on the left sleeve of their uniforms in 1923, but the experiment didn't even last to the end of the season. By 1932 all major league teams followed the Yankees' lead. In 1939, after Gehrig was diagnosed with ALS, the Yankees established another trend by permanently retiring his number 4.

Yankee Stadium, June 22, 2005

	1	2	3	4	5	6	7	8	9	R	H	E
Tampa Bay	0	0	0	2	0					2	5	0
Yankees	2	0	0	0	1					3	3	1

Pavano's sixth strikeout victim was Damon Hollins who led off the fifth. A hit batter and Nick Green's single put runners at the corners. Up stepped Crawford, who for the second time grounded to Robinson Cano, who flipped the ball to Jeter at second, who then threw to Russ Johnson at first for an inning-ending double play. Ah, the DP, a pitcher's best friend, a two-for-one bargain, and a rally-killer. It is always a great to see when the Yankees are on the field.

New York broke the tie in the bottom of the inning. Ruben Sierra got things started with a double to left centerfield. Kazmir then hit Johnson, and catcher John Flaherty's sacrifice put runners at second and third with one out. I was talking to my son-in-law Jonathan during the rally; soon after we said our goodbyes, Cano's grounder gave the Yankees the lead. I wished we would have talked longer, so he could have heard the cheers, but I don't know if the Astros fan would have enjoyed them. I sure did.

There was more excitement when Derek Jeter stepped up to the plate with Johnson just 90 feet away at third, but Jeter barely tapped the ball and was thrown out at first by catcher Toby Hall.

My Favorite Yankee Third Basemen

My favorites at the hot corner are Clete Boyer and Graig Nettles.

Mantle said he never saw anyone, including Brooks Robinson, play third as well as Boyer. He was the third baseman of my youth. I remember being with a friend, on opening day of the 1964 Fall Classic. When Ken Boyer stepped up to the plate, Bobby McNamara (a Cardinals fan) yelled, "Mom, it's Ken Boyer versus Clete Boyer." Older brother Ken and his team won the Series, but Clete had already won my heart. Playing third base during my first few years of team ball, I always pretended I was Clete Boyer.

Nettles drew a lot of praise for his work at third during the World Series. He also had some great quotes, like "I always wanted to play baseball and be in the circus. Playing with the Yankees, I got to do both." Another quote from Nettles was just moments before the crowd at Fenway was silenced that October day in 1978; he was saying to himself, "Pop it up, pop it up...not to me, not to me." He caught Yazstremski's fly and Gossage's embrace. A few days later, the Yankees hoisted another championship banner.

NEW YORK, NEW YORK

"Start spreading the news, I'm leaving today
I want to be a part of it–New York, New York…
If I can make it there, I'll make it anywhere
It's up to you—New York, New York."

—Fred Ebb and John Kander

NEW YORK CITY has been called the Big Apple, Gotham City, Metropolis, Spin City, and a number of other names, including simply, the City. It is so big that it encompasses five boroughs, is home to over eight million residents, and daily welcomes millions of commuters and tourists. Some say, "The place is so nice, you have to say it twice." New York, New York.

Call it whatever you want, but be sure you call it America's greatest city and the world's most famous. What a place! There is so much in New York City. The best of everything can be found in its environs.

Fitting that it would be home of the greatest sports team in the world.

Many have sung about New York, visited it, lived there, wished they lived there, and died there. I don't know how it became what it is today, but I have my ideas. Its history, shopping, restaurants, theaters, music, media outlets, and financial centers are without equal. New York is home to special places like the Rockefeller Center, Radio City, Coney Island, Wall Street, Times Square, Central Park, Broadway, and the Statue of Liberty. The City boasts many famous buildings, such as the United Nations building, the Empire State Building, St. Patrick's Cathedral, the Chrysler Building, and, of course, Yankee Stadium. There are the annual events, including New Year's Eve in Times Square, Macy's Thanksgiving Day Parade, the United States Open tennis tournament, fireworks on the 4th of July, the New York City Marathon and Nathan's Hot Dog Eating Contest. All are known around the world. The City is hustle and bustle, always open, activities 24/7, something for everyone. There's no place like it. Just thinking about it all makes the statement "faster than a New York minute" seem very appropriate.

As a baseball fan, and especially a Yankees fan, I agree with those who suggest that the three most important spots in New York, the must-see places for every visitor, are the

Statue of Liberty, the Empire State Building, and Yankee Stadium. I went to each one, saving the best for last. I was a part of it. I made it there. New York, New York: it's the place where my dream came true.

There may be as many reasons to enjoy New York as there are people who live there. To me, the greatest reason is the Stadium. For years I would not have even wanted to go to New York, in spite of its greatness, unless I could get to that famous structure in the south Bronx.

Three years before my visit to New York, my son Joshua passed through there twice. It was during the semester when he studied in Athens, Greece. He took field trips to many of the places where the apostle Paul had travelled to and preached. Joshua and his classmates visited parts of ancient Athens and the Greek isles, Florence, the Egyptian pyramids, and western Turkey. When the semester ended, he and some friends traveled to Paris, stopped to visit cities in Italy and Germany, as well as Spain, and eventually England before flying back to the USA. I asked him if by chance his plane flew over Yankee Stadium, and if it did, what he thought of seeing it from the air. It didn't. He didn't.

I figured it must have been a little disappointing to see all those places in Europe and fly in and out of JFK airport twice without seeing the Stadium. He didn't see the one place I desired to see more than any other place on earth. What's worse, he didn't care. I raised a Braves fan.

I have seen many beautiful places. I grew up at the foot of Pikes Peak, and the beauty of the Colorado mountains surpasses most places I have seen. Later I lived three blocks from the Atlantic Ocean and enjoyed the beaches and ocean view for over four years. I have seen the Bavarian Alps and the Rhine River valley. I have seen Niagara Falls, the Grand Canyon, the great redwoods of California, and the Smokey Mountains in Tennessee. I have seen the best of God's creation. As for man's work, I have seen the beautiful Neuschwanstein Castle in southern Germany, the Golden Gate Bridge, Mt. Rushmore, the Seattle Space Needle, and the Capitol building in D.C. But I wouldn't trade my visit to New York, and especially Yankee Stadium, for any of those places.

Others who visit New York go for reasons very different from mine. They want to take in a show on Broadway or to hear music at Carnegie Hall. In the winter they might want to see the Christmas tree or to skate at the Rockefeller Center. Many go to the City for the shopping and the restaurants. Those with political and international interests might go to the UN building, and no doubt millions will go to One World Trade Center. My mom was disappointed when she heard I didn't visit "Ground Zero."

"Green Acres" was a popular, albeit corny, sitcom in the 60s. It was part of my family's regular television viewing. I loved Fred Ziffel and his pig Arnold, the sell-anything Mr.

Haney, the store owner Sam Drucker, the confused county agent Hank Kimball (my favorite), and the Douglas's farm hand Eb Dawson. The silly song at the beginning still replays in my head. After my visit, I understand Mrs. Douglas singing, "New York is where I'd rather stay. I get allergic smelling hay. I just adore a penthouse view. Darling, I love you, just give me Park Avenue."

Gotham was also the home of Batman, Superman, and Spiderman, all titans in their own fictional ways. In professional sports, besides the Yankees and Mets, New Yorkers get to cheer for the Knicks and the Nets, the Rangers and Islanders, and the Giants and Jets. Plus there are the Liberty, the Red Bull, and New York City FC. For the sports fan, seldom does a day pass without there being at least one game involving one of the City's professional teams.

The best of everything can be found there, and the best of the best—the Yankees and Yankee Stadium—are there. And I was there.

There is evidence showing that baseball was called the national pastime as far back as the 1850s. Historians have various opinions about the beginning of baseball. Some say it evolved from the English games of cricket and rounders. Others say "town ball" was part of its origin. All three, with many variations, included someone with a bat trying to hit a ball and then running to a base or bases until he was called out. Many towns and cities had their own style and rules, but the one that set the stage for much of what we call baseball today was called "The New York Game."

There should be no surprise that the most significant city in America, boasting the greatest sports stadium in America with the greatest team in America would lend its name to what we now call baseball. The New York Game changed the square field with a diamond and replaced plunking with the tag and force plays. The New York Game, in contrast to other versions, introduced fair territory inside the baselines of the diamond. (Other games allowed for the ball to be hit in any direction.) Other innovations included having nine players on each team, allowing three outs per team at bat, and playing games lasting nine innings. Two additional aspects leaving a permanent mark on modern baseball came from the Massachusetts game: one was the overhand pitch and the other was to record an out by catching the ball before it hit the ground, no longer counting a one-bouncer as an out.

For over 50 years, New York was home to three major league baseball teams. In the early years of the 20th Century, the Giants were by far the best of the three and one of the best in all of baseball. But the Yankees with Ruth and Gehrig established themselves as the best team in the 1920s, a designation that stuck for nearly 40 years. The Yankees rise to prominence coincided with the Giants' fall. Until signing Jackie Robinson in the mid 40s, the Dodgers were the losers, dem Bums, and the "wait-til-next-year" team. Then came the "Era" (so called in Roger Kahn's excellent book, *The Era, 1947–1957: When the Yankees, the Giants, and the Dodgers Ruled the World*) which saw at least one of the New York teams in the World Series every year but one. The Yankees played in all but two years, meeting the Dodgers six times and the Giants once. The Giants played in one other fall classic during the stretch.

During the 50s, the New York teams boasted three of the best centerfielders in baseball, each having backers who claimed their centerfielder was the best. Baseball fans living in those years and experiencing the rivalries appreciated Terry Cashman's 1981 song, "Talkin' Baseball," a nostalgic look at the decade. Included in the lyrics are "Willie, Mickey and the Duke," repeated no less than seven times in the song. Mays, Mantle, and Snider were a trio of superstars, each one a centerfielder, and each one playing in New York at the same time.

Then, after the 1957 season, the Giants and Dodgers packed up and moved to California. The City which boasted three of the best teams in baseball all of a sudden had only one team. Many were brokenhearted at the departure of the Dodgers and Giants. Then, in 1962, along came the Mets, one of the worst teams in baseball history. The Amazing Mets were known as the "Loveable, Laughable, Losers." But non-Yankee fans, longing for a local team to root for, accepted the Mets and supported them in amazing ways. By decade's end, the Yankees were a second-division team and the Mets were world champions (1969). The Mets went to the Fall Classic again in 1973 and won it in 1986, but would not go again until 2000. With two teams playing in New York, the Yankees won six titles (1962, 1977, 1978, 1996, 1998, 1999) before facing the Mets in that 2000 World Series, which was the first Subway Series in 44 years.

Yankees fans may be the best and the worst. One thing is certain: they are knowledgeable of the nation's pastime and appreciative of Yankee history. A team's success can foster impatience in the fans, and when retiring stars are replaced, spectators might boo and criticize the new players. Mantle knew that. In the first decade of his career, he was frequently booed, even after his 1956 triple crown year, because he never measured up to manager Casey Stengel's claim that Mantle was Ruth, Gehrig, and DiMaggio rolled into one. It won't be easy for the next Yankee shortstop after Derek Jeter's long run in pinstripes.

When Roger Maris joined the Yankees all of a sudden the boos were directed at the man who would hit 61 homers in 1961, breaking Ruth's record. Mantle was finally treated like he deserved, and the fans began to adore him, standing every time he stepped up to the plate.

Although Yankee fans celebrate loudly when the team wins, they are tough on the players when they don't perform. Before I journeyed to the Stadium, Adam Hudson, the man with whom I stayed while visiting New York, commented on baseball fans, suggesting that Yankees fans are very knowledgeable. He opined, "If you go to a Mets game, you will likely talk about the weather, fashion, and the shows. But when you go to the Stadium, you talk stats, history, and baseball. It's not a social thing to go to Yankee Stadium. It's all baseball." Perhaps an overstatement, but he is not alone in his opinion.

I remember watching an episode of "Who Wants to be a Millionaire?" when a baseball question was asked. The contestant was stumped and used his "ask the audience" lifeline after the question, "Which MLB team changed its name during part of the 50s because of communism?" An amazing 95% of that audience answered, "the Reds." I was impressed; those New Yorkers knew their baseball. They must have been Yankee fans.

New York is a place where success is not easy to find. Not everyone makes it there. There is intense pressure to succeed, and many aspiring actors, writers, business people, and athletes, including some who have achieved success before arriving in the Big Apple, have succumbed to the stress. Goose Gossage struggled early in his first season in pinstripes, but he settled down and established himself as one of the game's premier relievers, helping the Yankees win the Series during that first year. He knows what it means to be sized up, analyzed, and criticized by New Yorkers. During the 1980 ALCS, while trying to protect a 2-1 Yankees lead, he gave up a massive home run to George Brett, which helped the Kansas City Royals sweep the Yankees and go on to the World Series. Reflecting on the loss, Gossage said he wept after the game—not because he was embarrassed by Brett's home run, but because he had let down his teammates and fans. "What I had difficulty with was losing. New York is a city of winners. The Yankees were a group of players who played to win. Anything less left everyone devastated."

Arriving on a Monday at the Newark airport, I looked to the east, and my eyes beheld the Empire State Building, the largest building in the city until One World Trade Center was completed. The next day I took the Harbor Cruise around the island, saddened that the twin towers were no longer standing, amazed at the Brooklyn and Manhattan bridges, awed by the United Nations buildings, and then deeply touched as we slowly approached Liberty Island to get a close up of the Statue of Liberty. Later I took the test to audition for the "Who Wants to be a Millionaire?" show.

In the middle of all these activities, I meandered along the streets of the City, amazed at the parks, the buildings, the stores, and the people. There were tourists everywhere, multiple foreign languages being spoken, amazement on the faces, and bags filled with souvenirs. Except for the languages, all of these descriptions were me. I looked for Brazilians, hoping to speak Portuguese and be like those of other nations, but didn't find any. The noise surprised and impressed me. It wasn't wildly loud, but it actually seemed to be quiet. Maybe I was just so locked in to my world of joy that I was deaf to much of the sounds nearby. I think I only heard but one or two car horns in spite of seeing many taxis. The City wasn't scary, and it didn't have unpleasant aromas like I thought there would be, especially while walking to the port.

I had no problem riding on subways, and the people seemed friendly everywhere I went. It reminded me of a scene in *Crocodile Dundee* when the Aussie first arrived in New York. He thought the people must be really friendly if that many lived in one "town." In a restaurant, I thought I had either lost my wallet or had it stolen. When I got ready to pay, I was so embarrassed, thinking I'd better get ready to wash dishes, but the manager came up and said, "No problem. Your dinner is free." I thanked him several times. Then, as I was about to leave, I noticed it was in my shirt pocket. I don't remember putting it there, neither on that day nor any other day for that matter. I paid for the dinner and thanked him again. He smiled and said, "If you liked your experience here, please come again." Next time I'm in New York I plan to visit Café Fiorello.

The favorite part of my shopping experience in New York was at the Yankees Clubhouse on 42nd Street. It was like entering a museum of ancient artifacts. I saw pictures, books, bats, uniforms, and much more. They were all highly priced and had an even higher price tag if they were autographed. Signatures of Yankees were everywhere. I bought a Yankees jacket and several other items, all from the non-autographed section. I spent over $100 of my long-saved New York spending money.

I took a closer look at my pictures after returning from New York. In one of the pictures, there is a building that I hadn't noticed while at the Stadium. It stands out, large and impressive, especially in the pictures I took while sitting directly behind home plate in the top row. It must be a 10-story building, probably larger. For three years, every time I looked at the 15 windows on the highest level on that building, I longed for the opportunity to work there so I could gaze upon the Stadium every day. I wouldn't have gotten much work done, but it would've been fun, especially if I were the boss.

Several times I heard my dad talk about the northeastern part of the United States. He never used kind words. I remember him saying, "Once you get into Ohio and throughout Pennsylvania and New York you see the worst of Americans. They are so rude." (That's the cleaned up version.) But that wasn't my experience. Of course he was driving an 18-wheeler on crowded highways, while I was there fulfilling a dream. Maybe I'm naïve, blind, or deaf, or maybe I chose to remember the best of what I observed. And what I saw in New York, New York, was something wonderful to behold.

"New York, New York" was the theme song in the 1977 Martin Scorcese film by the same name. The song was composed by John Kander with lyrics by Fred Ebb. Liza Minnelli performed the song in the movie, but the song didn't become popular until Frank Sinatra began singing it a year after the film's debut. It has since become the theme song of the City and has taken its place in Yankee lore. Now it is heard through the Yankee Stadium sound system immediately following every game. Sinatra's recording is played after a victory, and Minnelli's version airs after a loss. I heard her sing after the game; despite the loss and in spite of the rain, it was refreshing.

I made it there, to New York City. What a spectacular place. To borrow a New England description, it was "wicked cool."

Yankee Stadium, June 22, 2005

	1	2	3	4	5	6	7	8	9	R	H	E
Tampa Bay	0	0	0	2	0	0				2	5	0
Yankees	2	0	0	0	1	0				3	4	1

Pavano made quick work of the Rays in the sixth. From the three batters he faced, there were two ground outs and a pop fly. He had made just one mistake over six innings, but he was keeping his team in the game, leading 3-2. He had struck out six and was in superb control while bringing his fastball consistently at 92-94. It was one of his finest showings since signing a big contract with the Yankees during the off-season. For six innings, it had been one of his finest days at the Stadium. Things were about to change for him, however, and not just in the seventh inning.

In their half of the sixth, the Yankees squandered an excellent chance to increase their slim lead. Bernie Williams led off with a walk and Gary Sheffield singled to left, before Alex Rodriguez flew out to center. Hideki Matsui then moved the runners up with a ground out to Kazmir. Ruben Sierra was intentionally walked to load the bases, but the rally ended when first baseman Russ Johnson, who started that game with both Jason Giambi and Tino Martinez on the bench, flew out to right.

The inning was over, and I was disappointed. I wanted to see a power hitter like Giambi or Martinez pinch hit with the bases loaded. It didn't matter to me that it would have been lefty-against-lefty. Even though a manager usually won't use his only extra catcher this early in a game, I thought the switch-hitting Jorge Posada, also benched that day, was a better choice than Johnson. I wanted a home run threat up to bat in that situation. I knew 45,000+ would have been on their feet with me, cheering and anticipating every pitch. But Joe Torre, who didn't see things the way I did, was paid a lot of money to make those decisions. I wondered what the Boss, who was signing those checks, thought about Torre's decision.

My Favorite Yankee Shortstops

I know Phil Rizzuto was a popular player in his day, and both Mickey Mantle and Bobby Murcer originally played shortstop. But I never saw any of them play the position. I liked both Tony Kubek and Phil Linz, the latter because he wore glasses like I did. I saw them play with Mantle, but neither of them reached my "favorites" list. Bucky Dent did. He was traded at the beginning of 1977, one year before Gossage joined the Yankees. They were drafted by the White Sox and began playing together the same year. Dent played on back-to-back World Series winners.

Probably Dent's greatest moment in baseball, the most-memorable one anyway, is the one that made him famous (or, infamous, depending on which side of the Yankees-Red Sox rivalry one is on). It happened in the seventh inning of the 1978 playoff game in Boston when Dent silenced the Red Sox faithful with a three-run, go-ahead homer at Fenway Park. The shot was both a game changer and a name changer. Boston fans gave him a new middle name, and the dents on the Green Monster are now called dimples.

My other favorite Yankee shortstop is Derek Jeter. He was to many young ball players what Mantle was to my generation. Many copied his batting stance, wanted to wear his number, and tried to play shortstop. Like Mantle, Jeter was a hero from his first year. He was a gamer and a team-player, and he preferred to let his action on the field speak for him. He handled well the pressures of playing in New York, and he was a winner. And another similarity with the Mick: he loved being introduced by Bob Sheppard.

Jeter's rookie year concluded with the first of four World Series titles in a five-year span. He led his team to two more Series in the next three years. Then he earned another ring after leading the Yankees to their 27th championship in 2009. He finished his career with a .310 batting average while wearing pinstripes for 20 years. Cooperstown will be calling after the five-year waiting period is up.

Another "sure thing" with Jeter, and it won't take five years for this, is that his Number 2 will be retired and added to the group of retired Yankee numbers that will never be stitched on another pinstriped shirt. Since Joe Torre's Number 6 was retired, only one number remains between 1 and 10. That's "number 2, Derek Jeter." I can hear Sheppard's voice.

PLAYING CENTER FIELD
IN YANKEE STADIUM

*"To play eighteen years in Yankee Stadium is the
best thing that could ever happen to a ballplayer."*

—Mickey Mantle

ON MAY 21, 1954, Mickey Mantle hit the 61st home run
of his career. There were over 30,000 fans at the Stadium
that day. Mantle's home run to right field came off Frank
Sullivan in the eighth inning. Sullivan was making his first
career start for the Boston Red Sox.

Earlier that day, in a hospital halfway across America,
my mother gave birth to her fourth child. On the same
day that Yankee fans cheered a Mickey Mantle home run
in "The House that Ruth Built," mom and dad celebrated
in Iowa City the birth of their only child who grew up to
be a Yankees fan. If I could have, I would have clapped

– 129 –

for Mantle that evening. It was a nice way for him to welcome me into the world. I never stopped being a fan; he has always been my favorite.

The Mick launched three more "Happy Birthday, Ron" homers, in 1956, 1963, and 1967. He announced his retirement from baseball at the beginning of spring training in 1969. His last baseball card, the 1969 Topps #500, mentions his retirement. I have had it since 1969 when I paid a nickel for five cards and a stick of gum. It is not for sale, and it never will be. He is listed at 6 feet and 194 pounds. Although I am three inches taller and about 20 pounds heavier, I can't imagine myself being larger than he was. Mantle was small compared to today's home run sluggers, yet few if any in baseball history hit longer home runs than he did. He lives on as a giant of a man, a solid oak tree, a granite rock, and a Titan fitting of New York and comparable to the Empire State Building.

Dreams Do Come True: A Lifelong Yankees Fan Visits the Stadium

The author examines part of his collection of Mantle memorabilia. In the lower right corner is the 1969 Topps card that announced his retirement.

Yankee heroes never fade away. There are constant reminders of their greatness, in places like pictures, books, shirts, and monuments. This was evident in my walking around Manhattan and being at Yankee Stadium. In the Yankees Clubhouse on 42nd Street, in Modell's Sporting Goods, and in other stores, I saw more Mantle shirts and memorabilia than other Yankees, past or present. At the Stadium, I along with many fans, young and old, stood in front of Mantle's number and monument, posing for pictures. Yankees fans will not let Mantle be forgotten.

Authors, too, find interested fans who are ready to spend money and anxious to read about the Mick. David Falkner's *The Last Hero: The Life of Mickey Mantle* was released only a few months after Mantle's death on August 13, 1995. It was my son Josh's fourteenth birthday. Several additional books have been written since, including two of my favorites: Tony Castro's *Mickey Mantle: America's Prodigal Son* (2002) and Jane Leavy's *The Last Boy: Mickey Mantle and the End of America's Childhood* (2010). Both mention the impact Mantle had on a generation of fans, and both give a sobering commentary on Mantle's life off the baseball field. Years earlier, I had learned about Mantle's life, which broke my heart and cracked my naïve image I had had of my baseball hero. The books don't shy away from the way he lived his life, mentioning numerous events when he didn't act like the hero we considered him to be. But readers and fans like me need to be reminded of the imperfections of people and the dangers of placing too high of a value on humans.

Another great read is *Mickey and Willie* (2013), Allen Barra's book, which shows some amazing comparisons between the lives of the two great center fielders. Wonderful and exciting times were the 50sand 60s when the two future Hall of Famers, who combined for 1,196 home runs, began playing just a few blocks apart. Mays wowed the Giants fans at Manhattan's Polo Grounds while Mantle amazed Yankees fans at the Stadium in the Bronx. Mays played his final game for the Mets in 1973, five years after Mantle's final game. Although forty-plus years have passed, evidence of their playing days is still in abundance.

Other constant reminders of Mantle are the baseball cards. His 1951 Topps rookie card continues to increase in value, as do his other cards. I was in Brazil when I first heard that old baseball cards were selling for big money. My sister sent me an article, which included a picture of Pete Rose's rookie card and its high value, which arrived soon after he had surpassed Ty Cobb on the all-time hits record and prior to being banned from baseball. I owned that card, and I thought I would make a fortune selling it and other cards I had protected in boxes for over 20 years. In 1989, I began selling most of my cards, adding about $1,000.00 to a bank account in need of money. Not a bad pay off, since my childhood investment was only about $15.00. My most treasured, the one I will never sell, is Mantle's final card. I have been offered over $300.00, and it is worth more than that now, but it will be given to Josh. Maybe he will keep it for a long time, as if it were Chipper Jones's rookie card.

Mantle was born October 20, 1931, in Spavinaw, Oklahoma. A few years later, his family moved to Commerce, a mining town in the northeast corner of the state. The depression and Dust Bowl Days had taken their toll on many Americans in that area. Mantle's dad Mutt and other relatives worked in the mines; many died early by contracting various diseases related to their work. The brevity of life was constantly in the back of Mantle's mind; he thought he too would be dead before his fortieth birthday.

Young Mickey was an outstanding athlete, excelling in football and basketball as well as baseball. But his dad, a former semi-pro pitcher, and granddad Charlie raised him to be a baseball player. They taught him to be a switch hitter, and he finished his career with the most home runs by any switch hitter in baseball history.

Yankee scout Tom Greenwade convinced the Mantles, both Mickey and Mutt, to sign a contract after high school. Actually, Mickey skipped his high school graduation so he could play a baseball game, and then signed that same evening. He played in the minor leagues for just two years before catching the eye of manager Casey Stengel. Going against the Yankee higher-ups, Stengel insisted on bringing the 19-year old to the majors at the start of the 1951 season. Mantle possessed the rare combination of speed and power. He was the opening day starter in right field, which fulfilled a dream that he had of playing for the Yankees in The House that Ruth Built.

He hit 13 home runs his rookie year while playing in 96 major league games. He also played 40 games with the

AAA Kansas City Blues, having been sent down to work on his swing and learn to relax and ease up a bit. After being recalled by the Yankees in late-August, Mantle was a fixture in right field as the Yankees won their third of five straight World Series. In Game 2 of the Fall Classic, Mantle tripped on a drain cover while chasing a fly ball hit by Willie Mays. Mantle watched the rest of the Series from a hospital room. The knee injury affected him during the remainder of his career.

Yankees fan André King is a former student of mine. When we met for the first time he gave me a Red Sox program from the 1951 season. The Yankees were at Fenway for a three game set, July 6-8. Top Red Sox players that year included Ted Williams, Johnny Pesky, Bobby Doerr, Dom DiMaggio, and Lou Boudreau. On the opposite page were the names Phil Rizzuto, Yogi Berra, Joe DiMaggio, Jerry Coleman, Billy Martin, manager Casey Stengel, and coach Bill Dickey. Nine of these men are in the Hall of Fame. There was another future Cooperstown inductee, rookie Mickey Mantle, listed as the right fielder, wearing uniform Number 6. He entered the game in the second inning of that July 8 afternoon game, coming in to run for Joe DiMaggio, and he played the rest of the game in right field. Just two weeks later, he was demoted to the minors. Whoever got the program and watched the game that day saw a great coming together of outstanding baseball players. I have that program now, and it is in a safe place.

Mantle's reputation of power preceded him to the big leagues, and it never waned. People stood in awe watching him take batting practice and said the sound of the ball coming off his bat was different from that of any other player. He had already amazed fans with eye-popping home runs, but on April 17, 1953, a new term was invented due to a massive home run. In Washington that day, Mantle's blast off Nationals pitcher Chuck Stobbs left the park and ended up, according to Yankees publicist Red Patterson, 565 feet from home plate. That home run created the "tape measure" description which would become the standard of long-distance home runs.

From 1952 until his final season in 1968, Mantle hit over twenty round-trippers in every season but three, two of which were seasons that he missed considerable playing time because of injuries. The other was his final season when he hit 18. He ended his playing days with 536 homers, which at the time, was the third most in MLB history. In 1956, he finally proved himself to be all that Stengel promised he would be. He led the league with 52 homers and 130 runs batted in while batting .353. Winning the Triple Crown in batting is rare; only three players have accomplished the feat since Mantle did. Even rarer is to lead both major leagues in those three categories, which

Mantle also did. He was named most valuable player that year, which was the first of three times he won the award. He was runner-up in three other seasons.

A few years ago I was in an antique mall, rummaging through stacks of *Life* magazines from the 50s and 60s. I stumbled upon a great find: the June 25, 1956, issue had Mantle's picture on the cover. I paid more than the twenty-cent cover price to buy the magazine. It is another great addition to my baseball collection. A photographic essay, entitled "A Prodigy of Power: Mickey Mantle Comes of Age as a Slugger" included 18 pictures. He was already known as a power hitter, and when he stepped to the plate, people weren't thinking that he might hit one out; rather, they were thinking that he might hit one of the longest home runs ever. The article also mentions that Mantle was batting near .400 at the time, and on pace to break Ruth's single-season home run mark. Earlier that summer Mantle hammered a ball that came only inches from being the only fair ball ever hit out of the Stadium. He came very close again in 1963. Both were tape measure shots, and another term was born, Mantlesque, to describe what had been previously known as Ruthian blasts.

Mantle's final marquee season came in 1964 when he hit 35 home runs. It was also his last appearance in the World Series, where he hit three more homers, finishing his career as the all-time home run king in World Series play with 18. Game two of that Series was on a Saturday. The Yankees had lost the opening game, but I was certain Mantle and the Yankees would come back. I was with my dad at Daniels Chevrolet in downtown Colorado Springs. When Mantle led off the second inning with a ground out to Dick Groat, one of the salesmen who worked with my dad began mocking Mantle and teasing me after the out because I had predicted a home run. In the bottom of the ninth inning, after we had gone home, Mantle's walk-off shot broke the Babe's record for career World Series home runs. The salesman later told my dad that he was glad I wasn't there when that happened. He deserved any of the razzing I might have given him.

Mantle played in the post season in all but two of his first 14 seasons; the Yankees were world champions seven times. He also was chosen for the American League All-Star team every year from 1953–1968; he hit two home runs in those games.

Mickey Charles Mantle was inducted into baseball's Hall of Fame in Cooperstown, New York, in 1974, five years after his retirement. There was never any doubt that he would be inducted in his first year of eligibility; he received more than 88 percent of the votes.

Under Mantle's name on his monument at Yankee Stadium are the words, "A Great Teammate." Players of all age and skill were shown respect by Mantle. Perhaps he welcomed the younger players because he was shy and felt out-of-place in the Yankee locker room during his rookie year. Or maybe it was because of the way he was treated poorly by Joe DiMaggio, whose final season was Mantle's first. Mantle never felt accepted by the Yankee Clipper.

I asked Lindy McDaniel, who joined the Yankees in July of Mantle's final season, what it was like to play on the same team with Mantle. McDaniel, who pitched for 21 years before retiring in 1975, was also a preacher whose faith in God was well-known. Off the field, Mantle and McDaniel lived very different lives, but Mantle "was never unkind to me," Lindy said. "He treated me special, like he did all the Yankee players." Although Mantle spent many nights partying before a game, he claimed it never affected him in a game. He didn't want to let down his team.

Also on Mantle's monument are these words: "A magnificent Yankee who left a legacy of unequaled courage." He played through injury, and he played hard all the time. Teammates were amazed at what it took just to get him ready to play each game, the therapy that followed, the pain he played through, and the lack of complaining that accompanied it all.

When our son Daniel was about seven or eight years of age, he, too, liked Mantle. Maybe he liked Mantle because he was my favorite player, or maybe because Daniel was fascinated by something he read in one of my books. He was supposed to do some reading on his own, so I suggested *Young Baseball Champions*, a book I read when I was about his age. The chapter about Mantle begins with the story of a boy, attending a Yankees game. "All around him in Yankee Stadium, people were clapping hands, stomping feet, and shouting out one name: 'Mickey! Mickey! Mickey!'" Daniel loved repeating Mickey's name. He read those words with excitement in front of his classmates while giving his book report. I remembered my excitement at that age. I was that crowd, cheering on my favorite player.

His was an outstanding career. People associate the name Mantle with baseball greatness. He played for the greatest team in baseball history, during the time of its greatest success. On the field his star shone brightly.

He was also well-known for his activity off the field.

I was disillusioned and disappointed the first time I read about Mantle's personal life and continue to be saddened each time I pick up another book about him. During his years in pinstripes, the media rarely reported "bad press" about an athlete's private life. But eventually, Mantle's off-the-field activities were documented. Excessive drinking, vulgar language, and womanizing characterized his playing years and continued after retirement when he was The Mickey Mantle Show, a star attraction at card shows, fantasy camps, and other baseball promotional events. Still, the fans came in droves seeking a word with the Mick, an autograph or a picture with him. He usually obliged, but sent many away with mixed feelings about the player and the person.

But underneath it all, when he was sober, he was a good and caring person. That came out during the final years of his life.

He used to say, "If I had known I would live this long I would've taken better care of myself." It was a sad statement from one who was liked and sought out by millions of aging men who remained young while Mantle was still alive. He thought he would be dead by age 40 because death came early to several Mantle men who worked in the mines near Commerce. He died at age 63, a few months shy of another birthday. He wasted many years because of excessive drinking. When he finally checked into the Betty Ford Clinic and got sober, it was too late to reverse the self-inflicted damage. Even though he received a liver transplant, it only extended his life by a few months. But his generous spirit once again was manifested as he encouraged many to become organ donors. The events leading up to his death gave a new chance on life for many.

In the summer of 2003, Bev and I traveled to Branson, Missouri, to celebrate our 25th wedding anniversary. She was kind enough to let me drive a few miles out of the way to visit Commerce, Oklahoma. Entering into this near ghost town of a place, I saw the high school baseball field, named after Mantle. Then I saw a billboard announcing that the land across from the diamond was the future home of the Mickey Mantle Baseball Museum. I began planning a return visit, but the plans for the museum never materialized.

Bev was a good sport about delaying our Branson arrival, practicing a true Christian spirit of turning the other cheek because when we travel, I rarely stop for anything but gas and food, and we usually take care of both, plus a visit to the bathroom, at the same place. She let me take pictures of these two places without any comment, but she did laugh a little when I asked her to take a picture of me standing beside a street sign at the corner of Mickey Mantle Boulevard and Commerce Avenue. A few years later, in *A Hero all His Life,* written by his wife and three sons, I saw a picture of Mantle standing at that same place, in front of those street signs. Bev and I drove to a small supply store and asked for directions to Mantle's boyhood home. The people didn't know where it was. Even more disgusting is that a couple of them acted as if they had never heard of him.

We then drove down Commerce's main street and stopped at a small store to ask directions. The lady at the counter, Mrs. Shouse, affirmed that she was a longtime resident of Commerce and knew Mickey. She knew him very well, as a matter of fact. I would later find out that her husband Ivan was on the board of the Mantle museum, and he introduced Mantle to his wife Merlyn.

We had a delightful visit. She told us where he lived as a boy and where he and Merlyn lived for a few years during the early 50s. Then she told me that she remembered a day in high school when Mantle was looking at a *Life* magazine article with pictures of Joe DiMaggio. She smiled as she told me, "Mick said, 'One day, I'm going to be playing centerfield in Yankee Stadium.'" I wonder how many times I said that. John Fogerty says it too in his "Centerfield," an inspiring song that excites me every time I hear it. I might not have said it often, but I frequently thought, "Put me in, coach; I'm ready to play, today…look at me, I gotta be, centerfield." These words frequently come to mind, especially in February when pitchers and catchers are about to report to spring training, and the words always make me think about Mickey Mantle.

I was crazy about Mickey Mantle when I was a boy. When I played in the outfield, I wanted to play in center field. Later I tried playing first base, and it was not a coincidence that it happened the same year the Yankees moved Mantle to first. I tried switch hitting, but just couldn't hit a fast ball from the left side. My number of choice, obviously, was 7.

Injuries often sidelined him. The first was in game two of the 1951 World Series. Three great New York center fielders were involved in the play. Willie Mays of the Giants hit the ball that Mantle went racing for. Just as Joe DiMaggio called for it, Mantle hit a drain cover and tore up his knee. Commenting on the play, Mantle said, "My whole career terminated almost on that one play,…I thought I'd broken my leg in two and my career was over right there…all of my other injuries, and I had them every single year, came from favoring that knee…so as far as I'm concerned that was the worst thing that could ever have happened to me."

When Mantle joined the Yankees as a rookie at the start of the 1951 season, he was given uniform Number 6. Outfielder Cliff Mapes began the season wearing Number 7. Mantle didn't want his number because numbers three (Ruth) and four (Gehrig) had been retired, and DiMaggio was wearing Number 5. Stengel had billed him as the combination of those three great Yankees. The pressure was too much for the shy, 19-year-old Oklahoman. After a poor start, he was sent to the AAA Kansas City Blues in mid-July, and infielder Bobby Brown was given Number 6. Two weeks later, Mapes was picked up by the St. Louis Browns, and his Number 7 was given to Bob Cerv, who had been playing with Mantle in Kansas City. But near the end of August Cerv was gone, and Mantle was called back to New York. The Mick was happy to be given Number 7. No Yankee has worn the number since.

Yankee Stadium, June 22, 2005

	1	2	3	4	5	6	7	8	9	R	H	E
Tampa Bay	0	0	0	2	0	0	3			5	6	0
Yankees	2	0	0	0	1	0	0			3	4	1

After giving up a lead-off walk, Pavano caught Reggie Taylor looking at strike three, then induced Damon Hollins to fly out to Williams in center. Two outs and things were looking good.

How quickly things change.

After hitting Toby Hall for the second time, Pavano fired a 1-ball, 2-strike pitch to light-hitting Nick Green, Tampa

Bay's number nine hitter. Green turned on it and blasted one of only 17 home runs in his career that included 1,220 plate appearances over eight seasons in the bigs. The ball went just beyond Sierra's grasp as he jumped at the wall; it was barely fair down the leftfield line. A stunned Yankee Stadium got real quiet as Green rounded the bases, and the Rays took a 5-3 lead. The silence was soon broken by boos as Pavano walked off the field, having made another mistake, his second gopher ball, the two E-1's were responsible for all of Tampa Bay's runs.

I was on the phone with Josh early in the seventh inning, feeling good about my day at the Stadium and the Yankees 3-2 lead. He said goodbye, and moments later, I was feeling good about my day at the Stadium but not about the 5-3 score.

Mike Stanton came on and got the final out, but there was a very different New York state-of-mind among Yankee fans.

Staked to a two-run lead, Kazmir had little difficulty retiring each of the three Yankees he faced to end his day's work. Through seven innings, he had surrendered just four hits and two walks while striking out four Yankees. He looked much better than his 2-5 record entering the game indicated. The Yankees' bats, so active the night before, had been considerably calmed by the rookie lefthander.

A GLORIOUS QUEST

"To dream the impossible dream...
to reach the unreachable star
This is my quest—to follow that star
no matter how hopeless, no matter how far...
And I know if I'll only be true to this glorious quest
that my heart will be peaceful and
calm when I'm laid to my rest.

—Joe Darion

WHAT A GLORIOUS quest! What a delightful pursuit! Yes, I made it. I reached for what had seemed to be an unreachable star for so long. But I caught up to it, grabbed on to it, and wouldn't let go of it. Many have found peace and calm because they were true to their glorious quest. I found it at Yankee Stadium. My heart still feels at ease when I think about the impossible dream that came true.

– 147 –

When I showed my ticket and walked through the turnstile, I was only a few steps from the seating area. I arrived, and my eyes were overcome with beauty as I joyfully surveyed the playing field and the bleachers. I stood in disbelief as my eyes beheld what my mind had wanted to see for 40 years. If anyone had been standing near me, I think I would have said the same words uttered by Ned Beatty in the movie *Rudy*. His character, Mr. Ruettiger, stood inside Notre Dame Stadium, fixed his eyes on the field, and said, "This is the most beautiful sight these eyes have ever seen."

Those were my thoughts. What made the Stadium special wasn't the structure but the Yankee players and the team's history. Both had been part of me for as long as I could remember. There was a game played there that day, but I felt like I was in a museum, a place where my heroes had played.

Yankee history is filled with heroes and championships. There are more Yankees enshrined in baseball's Hall of Fame (54) and more MVPs (22) who wore pinstripes than from any other team. The 27 championships surpasses the 11 won by the St. Louis Cardinals, second on the list. Among those with their plaques in Cooperstown are lifelong Yankees Lou Gehrig, Earle Combs, Bill Dickey, Joe DiMaggio, Phil Rizzuto, Yogi Berra, Mickey Mantle, and Whitey Ford. No doubt Derek Jeter will be next. Other Hall of Famers played only part of their careers with the

Yankees. Jack Chesbro, Babe Ruth, Waite Hoyt, Herb Pennock, Tony Lazzeri, Lefty Gomez, Red Ruffing, Joe Gordon, Johnny Mize, Reggie Jackson, Goose Gossage, Dave Winfield, Rickey Henderson, and Wade Boggs are among those who had great years with the Yankees and other teams.

Besides the players, managers Miller Huggins, Joe McCarthy, Casey Stengel, and Joe Torre are in the Hall, as are longtime executives Jacob Ruppert, Ed Barrow, Lee MacPhail, and George Weiss. George Steinbrenner also deserves to be there.

An interesting bit of trivia is that of all the former Yankees in the Hall, Dazzy Vance is the only one who played briefly in New York at the beginning of his career. Vance was a rookie with the Pirates before playing his second and only season as a Yankee.

So much history and boyhood desire came together that June morning when I saw the Stadium for the first time. I was in awe, I was grateful, and I was full of joy. When I was in elementary school, my mom often dropped us off at the West Side Library, just a few blocks from our house on 31st Street in Colorado Springs. If it weren't for the baseball books, I probably would have been run out for disorderly behavior. But I found those books, and I remember reading about Ruth, Gehrig, and DiMaggio. I doubt that I ever completely read or understood any book through

– 149 –

high school and even my first years of college, unless it had something to do with sports. Baseball kept my attention while other things did not. I learned about the early years of baseball, the champions, and the players who struggled to succeed. I have remembered most of those facts through the past 40 years

In my late 40s, I began to exercise regularly, doing a light cardio workout at one of the fitness centers in Lubbock. My workouts for four to five days a week included 20-40 minutes on a stationary bicycle. My doctors loved the physical results, and I enjoyed knowing my blood pressure and heart rate were good. And it was awesome to see bulging muscles in places where I didn't even know I had muscles. My greatest joy, however, has been the mental results. Because I was so bored riding that bike, I started bringing along books, baseball books, mostly. I have read more than 100 books in the past ten years. I have learned much more about baseball, especially some of the finer details of the game's history and players and of the New York Yankees.

Among the plethora of amazing pieces of information I have stumbled upon, is that baseball history is filled with countless events that almost never happened. Now I've never been one to pay much attention to the "what if" questions in life, but here are some that have had large and lasting effects on baseball, especially New York Yankee baseball.

The first "What If" of importance goes back to the very beginning of Yankees baseball. What if Ban Johnson had not insisted on there being an American League team in the Big Apple? He didn't think the new league would survive without one. Johnson was the founder and first president of the American League, which was the first league to successfully challenge the National League. It began in 1901 with eight teams. One of those, the Baltimore Orioles, went bankrupt after the 1902 campaign, and Johnson moved them to New York for the next season. The New York Giants and manager John McGraw were against the idea. If they had gotten their way and the Orioles stayed in Baltimore, then Ruth, Gehrig, DiMaggio, and Mantle would never have worn pinstripes. And Cal Ripken, Jr. might have ended up in St. Louis playing for the Browns, who eventually brought baseball back to Baltimore in 1954.

The New York American League team was originally called the Highlanders, although some media and fans mockingly called them the Porch Climbers and the Burglars. Within a few years, New York media began referring to the team as the Yankees, which in 1913 became the team's official name. If they were still called the Highlanders, however, maybe some Southerners would be more accepting of their greatness.

The team moved into the Polo Grounds in 1913, sharing the field with the Giants. Soon after the acquisition of

Babe Ruth, who walloped 148 home runs in his first three seasons in New York (1920–1922), the Giants gave notice to the Yankees to get out and play somewhere else.

Being told early in the 1922 season that they were being kicked out, Yankees owners Jacob Ruppert and Tillinghast L'Hommedieu Huston immediately went to work, finding land and construction workers to build what would become the greatest sports facility in America. It was just across the Harlem River in the Bronx, only a short distance from the Polo Grounds. It was built in 284 working days at a cost of $2.5 million, paid by Ruppert and Huston. The three-tiered Stadium originally included 60,000 seats, nearly 20,000 more than any other baseball park. The copper frieze, hanging from the roof of the grandstands, would become one of the Stadium's iconic symbols.

On opening day, April 18, 1923, a reported 74,217 fans crowded into the palace. The gates were closed 30 minutes before the game's first pitch, and more than 20,000 were not permitted to enter. New York Governor Al Smith threw out the ceremonial first pitch. The Seventh Regiment Band, directed by John Philip Sousa, played the national anthem. Babe Ruth homered in the first game, a 4-1 victory over the Boston Red Sox. In October that year, the Yankees won their first World Series championship, defeating none other than the New York Giants. McGraw was *not* happy.

It is difficult to imagine baseball without Yankee Stadium. I don't even want to consider "What if the Yankees had stayed at the Polo Grounds?"

The early field dimensions of Yankee Stadium, built for the left-handed swinging Ruth, included the short porch in right field, not that he needed it, because when Ruth was at the plate, the bleachers were never far away. In stark contrast, the distance to center field was an astonishing 500 feet from home plate and the left center field wall was 465 feet. If the field dimensions then were more like the field dimensions after 1975, Ruth's home run numbers probably wouldn't have changed much if at all. But a power hitting right-hander like Joe DiMaggio might have hit an additional ten home runs each year over his 13-year career. The switch-hitting Mantle, who always considered himself to have greater power swinging right-handed, believed he lost at least 100 home runs because of the dimensions in Yankee Stadium. Of course the lunging grab Mantle made on Gil Hodges's drive to left-center in Don Larsen's perfect game would have been a home run in nearly every other MLB park, but to Yankees fans, that's not important.

Another "What If" involves Ruth, the former Red Sox pitcher-turned-outfielder. It boggles the mind to imagine how baseball history would be rewritten were it not for Harry Frazee and his selling Ruth to finance *No, No, Nanette*. The Red Sox had won four championships from

1912–1918 (Ruth was a member of three of those teams), and were considered along with the Giants to be one of the two best teams in Major League Baseball. No telling how many more titles the Red Sox might have won with Ruth on their roster. With Ruth, the Yankees won four.

Carl Mays is the subject of another "what if." He won over 200 games pitching for the Red Sox, Yankees, and Reds. Perhaps he is best known in baseball for having thrown the pitch that struck Cleveland shortstop Ray Chapman, the only baseball player ever to die from an injury sustained in a game. That game, on August 16, 1920, was one of the saddest days in baseball history. During the previous year, Mays walked off the field during a Red Sox game in Chicago, drawing the ire of Ban Johnson. When the Red Sox sold Mays to the Yankees, Johnson was angry at both teams and suspended Mays. But the Yankees activated him anyway and he finished the season in New York. As a result, the American League nearly split into two factions; five teams agreed with Johnson, but the other three, including New York, were ready to join the National League to form a new twelve-team league. If that would have happened, the Yankees might have become the most successful team in the National League.

Babe Ruth and Lou Gehrig formed one of the greatest duos in sports history. Were it not for Ruth, Gehrig might have been the best Yankee ever. He was certainly the most beloved baseball player, establishing the mark of 2,130 consecutive games played before being stricken with amyotrophic lateral sclerosis (better known as "Lou Gehrig Disease") and dying of the disease just a few weeks before his 38th birthday. The streak began the day Gehrig entered a game as a pinch hitter. The next day, he started in place of Wally Pipp who had gotten hit on the head in batting practice. It is difficult to know when the streak might have begun, since for ten years Pipp had been the regular Yankee first baseman, and a good one at that. He batted near or over .300 for seven straight seasons before coming down with one of the biggest headaches in baseball history.

Another "What If" involves two very successful Californians, contemporaries who played in the Pacific Coast League before moving east to play in New York and Boston. Joe DiMaggio joined Gehrig and the Yankees in 1936 and helped the Yankees win four consecutive World Series titles from 1936–1939. One of baseball's greatest years—and I'm not even talking about the Yankees winning their ninth championship—was in 1941 when Joltin' Joe DiMaggio hit in 56 consecutive games, the record that many believe will never be broken. Ted Williams was a Red Sox rookie in 1939. All he wanted was to be known as "the greatest baseball hitter of all time," a statement that few would argue. In 1941, Williams compiled some of the best hitting statistics ever. While DiMaggio batted .408 during

– 155 –

his hitting streak, Williams hit .406 for the entire season, which included 143 games. No one has hit above .400 since. Neither Hall of Famer played at a user friendly home field.

DiMaggio played most of his games in a place where the longest distance from home plate was the power alley in left center field, where he typically hit the ball. Williams, batting left-handed in Fenway Park, also faced a distance of over 400 feet for his power stroke. One wonders what might have happened if Williams had worn pinstripes and DiMaggio played in Beantown with brothers Dom and Vince, who played there for 11 and two seasons, respectively. The switch nearly happened, but not early in their careers. Supposedly Larry MacPhail, Yankees part-owner and General Manager, and Boston owner Tom Yawkey were drinking together at Toots Shor's Restaurant, a favorite place frequented by celebrities in the 1940s and 1950s. MacPhail and Yawkey agreed on a trade, but when they sobered up the next morning, the deal was off. Yawkey was not about to send another superstar to the Yankees, but if it had have happened, both would have smashed more home runs to add to their career totals, especially Williams who played eight full seasons after DiMaggio's retirement.

Mickey Mantle is the principal player in many of the "What if this would have happened" scenarios. The first lingering situation involves his tripping over that drain cover during Game 2 of the 1951 Series. That knee injury slowed him down for the rest of his career.

There is also the question of "What if Mantle would have kept the Number 6 uniform?" Mantle and Number 7 go together naturally, but Mantle and Number 6 would have changed things. "Lucky 7" is a popular idea that has been around for a long time. The Bible uses seven in figurative language to describe perfection. Seven also goes with many notables, including the days of the week, the colors of the rainbow, the dwarfs, the wonders of the world, and the notes on the musical scale. Plus, my first granddaughter Abi was born at 7:52 a.m. on March 7, and weighed 7 pounds and 2 ounces. Mantle and 6 would have made things very different.

The greatest "What If" concerning Mantle was his own statement, "If I had known I was going to live this long, I would have taken better care of myself." If he had have taken better care of himself, maybe he would have played longer. And what if the designated hitter rule was in effect during his playing days? No doubt he would have played longer and smashed more balls into the hands of spectators in the outfield bleachers.

Probably the least important "What If" involving Mantle deals with singer/songwriter Paul Simon who, like me, was a Mantle and Yankees fan. In the song "Mrs. Robinson," made famous by the movie *The Graduate*, Simon wanted to use Mantle, not Joe DiMaggio, in the lyrics. But "where have you gone, Mickey Mantle" just didn't work as well as Joe DiMaggio, and there was no way to insert "The Commerce Comet has left and gone away" into the song.

The final "What If" involves Yankee Stadium and the fulfillment of my dream. During the late 60s and early 70s, attendance was down, the team was playing poorly, and crime was increasing in the area near the Stadium. There was talk of moving the Yankees to New Jersey where they would play in the new Hackensack Meadowlands sports complex, where the New York Football Giants (I miss hearing Howard Cosell say that) decided to go. I can't even think about the Yankees playing in New Jersey. I am ecstatic that never happened. Mayor John Lindsey has become one of my heroes since I read of his efforts to push for a new and improved Yankee Stadium. The Yankees made a 30-year agreement with The City to stay put until 2002. The old Yankee Stadium was gutted and completely renovated. For two seasons, 1974–1975, the Yankees shared Shea Stadium with the Mets. Many Yankee players and fans said the changes were so significant that the Stadium just wasn't the same, and it shouldn't be referred to as "The House that Ruth Built."

The changes didn't matter to me. So much remained, including the façade (albeit in a different place), the monuments (out of center field and in a special place off the playing field), the subway rails just beyond the right field bleachers, the location, and most of all, the memories of Yankees past. By the time that 30-year pact ended in 2002, owner George Steinbrenner had no thoughts about moving the Yankees out of the Bronx. A new home for the team, yes, but it would be built across the street from the field of my dreams. I followed that star and my quest was completed, and it was indeed a glorious quest.

Yankee Stadium, June 22, 2005

	1	2	3	4	5	6	7	8	9	R	H	E
Tampa Bay	0	0	0	2	0	0	3	0		5	6	0
Yankees	2	0	0	0	1	0	0	0		3	5	1

Tanyon Sturtze came in to face the Rays in the 8th and had no trouble getting three quick outs. The two-run deficit seemed easy to overcome as the Yankees came to bat in their half of the eighth inning. Down 11-7 the night before, they had pounded the Rays for 13 runs in the eighth. So, just score three runs to take the lead and bring in Mariano Rivera to close things in the ninth seemed both possible and likely since the heart of the Yankees order was coming to bat.

Scott Kazmir, the Mets' 2002 number one pick, was replaced after pitching seven innings and allowing just four hits. Reliever Lance Carter got Williams and Sheffield to fly out. When Alex Rodriguez singled to left, Piniella went to Danny Baez, who walked Matsui. A-Rod and Tony Womack, who came in to run for Matsui, and both advanced a base after a passed ball. A single would tie the score; a home run would explode the fuse that had been lit. We were on our feet, expecting more fireworks, but Baez struck out Sierra to end the inning.

There was just one more inning. No reason to worry, though. Everyone knows "It ain't over 'til it's over." And these were the Yankees, playing in Yankee Stadium, where dreams come true.

My Other Favorite Yankee Outfielders

My favorite Yankee outfielders, other than Mantle, are Roger Maris, Bobby Murcer, and Paul O'Neill.

Roger Maris: 61 in '61. Amazing. He was my friend Casey Elliott's favorite Yankee. We used to "compete" in my backyard (he was Maris, I was Mantle) in our own version of home run derby. Like Mantle, Maris was quiet and came from a small town. Unlike Mantle, Maris never felt comfortable playing and living in New York. He won back-to-back MVP awards in 1960 and 1961. His swing was as pure as any I have ever seen. He also had a strong arm and was a good base runner. It is a shame that so many never accepted him as the outstanding player he was. He was grateful to be traded to the Cardinals after the 1966 season and vowed never to come back to the Stadium. After years of pleading by former players and George Steinbrenner, Maris returned in 1978 and received a warm welcome.

Bobby Murcer was supposed to be the next Mantle. Many thought he was next in the line of great Yankee outfielders—Ruth, DiMaggio, and Mantle—to roam the green grass in the Yankee Stadium. He came to New York from Oklahoma as a shortstop, but like another great player from the Sooner State, he too was moved to center field. Murcer, like Maris, was a pull hitter. The short fence in Yankee Stadium was good to him, but the larger Shea

Stadium was not so inviting. After averaging nearly 26 home runs in his first five years with the Yankees, he hit just 10 in the one season he played at Shea. In 1975, he was traded to the Giants, then to the Cubs two years later, before returning "home" to the Yankees in the middle of 1979. He had something else going for him: along with his good friend Thurman Munson, he was to be part of the next M & M boys.

I was ready for Murcer to win my affection and become my next favorite Yankee. I imitated his stance and swing when I became a left-handed hitter. I was thrilled to get a call from him as I boarded the train, leaving Penn Station on the day I visited the Stadium.

Paul O'Neill was a grinder. He gave it his best effort every at bat and every time he chased a ball hit his way. He was focused and didn't accept failure. You have to admire a guy who strives to win the way he did. He didn't want to go to the Yankees, but his dad said it was a good thing. Eventually, he agreed with the title of the 50s sitcom, "Father Knows Best." O'Neill began his career in his hometown of Cincinnati and won a World Series ring, but he never hit above .276 in his six full seasons there. He joined the Yankees in 1993, and in the next nine years, he hit for a .303 average, knocked in 95 runs a year, and won four more rings.

Dreams Do Come True: A Lifelong Yankees Fan Visits the Stadium

After O'Neill's retirement, "The Warrior," as he was called by The Boss, wrote a very touching book, *Me and My Dad*. I remember him playing Game 4 of the 1999 Series, the same day he had learned earlier that his dad had passed away. Celebrating the four-game sweep of the Braves was far from his mind, and mine, too, as I observed the outpouring of emotion by O'Neill's teammates and fans. Another show of support was during his final game at the Stadium, Game 5 of the 2001 Series. Thinking O'Neill might be running off the Yankee Stadium turf for the last time, fans were calling his name and cheering wildly. But in the bottom of the ninth, for the second consecutive night, the Yankees tied the game with a ninth inning home run and then won the game in extra innings. O'Neill's two final games in New York were two more additions to the mystic and magic of the great Yankee Stadium.

PRICELESS!

Ticket to the Yankees game against the Rays ... $40.00
Riding the trains from Bridgewater to
the 161ˢᵗ Street exit ... $20.00
A program, foot-long Hebrew Union
hot dog, and large drink ... $18.75
Living the dream of being at Yankee
Stadium ... Priceless!

WEDNESDAY AFTERNOON AT 3:55 p.m., Derek Jeter took a final swing. He missed. Strike three. Ballgame. Just like that the game was over, and it was time to leave. I was sad about the final score, but I was in Yankee Stadium, living my dream. There was still joy in The House that Ruth Built. I was *not* in Mudville, at least not the place written about in Ernest Lawrence Thayer's "Casey at the Bat," which includes these words:

Oh, somewhere in this favored land,
The sun is shining bright;
The band is playing somewhere,
And somewhere hearts are light,
And somewhere men are laughing,
And somewhere children shout;
But there is no joy in Mudville—
Mighty Casey has struck out.

With Robinson Cano on third, the "mighty" Jeter struck out, but my joy of being at Yankee Stadium had not diminished in the least.

With a soft rain falling, most of the fans were in a hurry to leave. I took my time, taking a few more photos and walking slowly through the seating area. Cups and other pieces of memorabilia had been left, and I wanted to grab as much as I could carry. Like the garage sale slogan, one fan's trash is another fan's treasure. Stadium personnel didn't share my desire and asked me to leave. I took one long and final look and said goodbye to the playing field.

On my way to the subway station, I turned again to get another look at the outside walls. Then I faced the stairs and headed for the B-train to begin my way back to New Jersey. As I awaited the train's arrival, I reminisced about the events that had taken place since my arrival at 10:00 that morning. Along with what I saw there, I also remembered several of the dreams I had imagined of coming here. I was a mixture of a ten-year-old boy and a 51-year-old man. The day was far from over, but the seven hours of living my dream came to an end as the train slowly moved away from the platform at the 161st Street Exit, and the Stadium disappeared from sight. I was feeling like a kid at Six Flags who had the ride of his life, but when the roller coaster stopped, he had to dismount and walk away. I was sad, but mostly I was smiling, and it felt good.

I spoke with a few passengers on the trains and was happy to inform them that I had been inside Yankee Stadium. When my host picked me up in Bridgewater, I began filling him in on the day's events. I also spoke with several people after the church's mid-week Bible Study. Like the previous night, I had trouble falling asleep as my mind sought to relive every detail of that Wednesday, June 22, 2005, in the Bronx. Carol Burnett's words were fitting; she said, "When you have a dream you've got to grab it and never let go." I never let go of my dream, and I wasn't about to stop thinking about it any time soon.

Early the next morning, I was taken to Newark, and I boarded the first of two planes that would get me back to Lubbock. I had left one "home" to return to another home. I knew Bev would be waiting for me, and I couldn't wait to see her and tell her more of what happened the day before when my dream came true. And I also wanted to thank her for her love and patience. She probably thought I had acted childishly and irresponsibly, but if she did, she never let me know.

From its beginning in 1923 until the final game played there September 21, 2008, Yankee Stadium was a gold mine of history. And Eureka! I discovered it, too. Although it was built on a small ten-acre plot of land and has since been destroyed, to this lifelong Yankee fan, it is immense and spectacular.

Visiting Yankee Stadium: it really is priceless. And I'm not the only one who thinks this.

Jason Giambi knocked 209 home runs during his seven years with the Yankees. After playing in the final game at Yankee Stadium, he said, "This is a place where men become children and think about their heroes, and where children always remember as men. It gets passed on from generation to generation about how these memories live on." Giambi's dad, a Yankee fan, was filled with wonderment when his son signed with the Yankees.

In the summer of 2008, Hall of Famer Frank Robinson was interviewed on Fox Sports; he told Chris Rose, "It's just a pleasure always, and I always look forward to coming to Yankee Stadium. All the history that they have, and all the great players that played there, and the mystique of the Yankee teams and the pinstripes and all of that. You're in awe the first time you step onto those grounds. It's like they're holy."

In an article on the Yankees website, published on September 19, 2008, Hal Bodley wrote, "The first time I walked into Yankee Stadium, I was in awe. No, make that giddy. If there's an unknown emotion lurking inside, the old ballpark has a way of bringing it out. It's always been that way. The grass is greener at Yankee Stadium, the baseball more important and the paying customers more intense. No matter the occasion, there's urgency when you enter."

Two days after I read Bodley's comments, the final game was played at Yankee Stadium. Andy Pettitte was the winning pitcher in the 8-3 triumph over the Orioles. Mariano Rivera pitched the ninth inning. Catcher Jose Molina hit the final home run. I can still hear an excited Jon Miller making the call: "That ball is deep. *Adiós*."

Derek Jeter grew up cheering for the Bronx Bombers, and all he ever wanted to do was play shortstop for the New York Yankees, something he did for 20 years before retiring after the 2014 season. On the final night at The House that Ruth Built, the Captain addressed the adoring fans who were in no hurry to leave. "There's a lot of tradition, a lot of history, and a lot of memories [here]," he began. "Now the great thing about memories is you're able to pass it along from generation to generation. And although things are going to change next year—we're going to move across the street—there are a few things with the New York Yankees that never change: it's pride, it's tradition, and most of all, we have the greatest fans in the world."

I will always be one of those fans.

Yankee Stadium, June 22, 2005

	1	2	3	4	5	6	7	8	9	R	H	E
Tampa Bay	0	0	0	2	0	0	3	0	0	5	6	0
Yankees	2	0	0	0	1	0	0	0	0	3	6	1

Sturtze had another 1-2-3 inning, and one of life's most thrilling and agonizing moments was coming up. It was the bottom-of-the-ninth.

There was just one more at bat for the Yankees. Trailing 5-3, they would at least get a chance to win the game. The Yankees had their work cut out for them as they faced a strong young right-hander in Baez, who would finish the season with 41 saves. The task, however, was not insurmountable. This is baseball, where there is no "taking a knee" or "running out the clock." In baseball, you always get your final at bat in the ninth, and there are always three outs before the game is over.

The moment had come. For 25 Yankees, their coaches, and 48,000+ spectators, hope was still alive. One 51-year-old fan, sitting in Section M16, Row H, Seat 22, was filled with expectation of another Yankee win. But even if the victory were to elude the Yankees, I would not have been disappointed. I was at the field of my dreams. I was in Yankee Stadium. I was watching my favorite team. I was a Yankee. I was living out my dream of dreams and enjoying every moment of it. A win was desirable, but the outcome was not going to diminish my joy. No, not on this day, for I had already received all that I had dreamed about.

It looked good for the Yanks as Joe Torre had plenty of bench strength ready, and they were able to change the score. The Voice, Bob Sheppard, introduced two pinch hitters—first Jorge Posada and then Jason Giambi—to begin the ninth. This must have sent fear into the Rays (Posada had homered and Giambi singled and doubled the previous night). It certainly excited Yankees fans. Neither Yankee, however, reached base.

We still had one out left, and nothing could take that away from us. When Robinson Cano tripled to left center and Jeter, the captain, fan favorite, and latest "Mr. Clutch" came to the dish, fans were standing, cheering, and expecting the game to last at least one batter after him. But the law of averages won this time. Even the best fail to reach base the majority of the times they step into the batter's box. On this day, the majority won as Jeter struck out. It was the second time in this game that he was retired with a runner on third. It turned out that this was one of six times in June that Jeter came to the plate as the tying, winning, or go-ahead run but made the game's final out. Even so, fans love the guy. He has taken a place among Yankee greats with Ruth, Gehrig, DiMaggio, Berra, and Mantle. The next clutch hit in him would have to wait. Surely the Yankees will retire Number 2, and he will get a call from Cooperstown in 2020. But on the day after hitting three singles, a double, and a homer, he walked off the field without affecting the score. There were no boos showered down on Jeter, but there were some drops of a late afternoon rain.

With the loss, the Yankees' record dropped to 37-34. They were in third place, five games out of first. But the loss was to the Rays who at 25-47 were twelve and one-half games behind New York. Plus, Rays manager Lou Piniella had previously managed the Yankees, and George Steinbrenner did not like losing to his former employees. Joe Torre's job was once again in jeopardy. No doubt Steinbrenner was mulling over the idea of another managerial firing, but fortunately Torre stayed around, which was a good decision, no doubt about it.

Other Yankee Favorites

I spent three summers introducing players when they came to the dish. I got the job through the recommendation of Steve Cervi, my high school journalism teacher. He has a great voice (still does public address work for high school and college games in Colorado), and I thought mine was a close second. Neither of us compared, however, with "The Voice," Bob Sheppard. His first game was April 17, 1951, which marked the beginning of two great careers at Yankee Stadium: his and Mickey Mantle's. Sheppard said his favorite name to announce, the most "poetic," as he put it, was Mickey Mantle. Mantle said, "Every time he announced my name, I got shivers up my back."

For more than fifty years, he was "The Sheppard of the Yankees Flock." On May 7, 2000, he was honored with a plaque in Monument Park. He continued to announce games for another seven seasons. In 2010, he passed from this life at the age of 99. He was honored for "the dignity that he brings to the baseball park, the seriousness with which he takes his job, and his ability to gain absolute perfection."

Derek Jeter said, "I think we have the best announcer in baseball, and I get chills every time I hear him." The chills must have continued, even after Sheppard's retirement, because Jeter had Sheppard's introduction taped, so it could be played every time he came to bat wearing pinstripes.

I don't remember when Casey Stengel managed the Yankees (my first memory of him is when he skippered the Amazin' Mets), but I have read things about him that amaze me. Many were shocked that this long-time loser (he had little success as a player; in nine seasons as manager with Brooklyn and the Boston Bees/Braves, he had only one winning record) was hired by the Yankees before the 1949 campaign. He was considered by many to be a clown, but opinions changed when he led the team to a record five consecutive titles.

After the streak ended in 1953, the Yankees went back to the Series five more times in the next seven years, winning two. After losing to the Pirates in 1960, Stengel was fired. The Yankees announced that he was too old to manage at age 70. To that the Ol Perfesser quipped, "I'll never make the mistake of being 70 again."

He was one of the first to platoon players, something that helped the switch-hitting Mantle. He seemed to get the best out of players past their prime, like Johnny Mize and Enos Slaughter. His selection of pitchers was often questioned but usually proved to be brilliant, like his choosing Don Larsen to pitch Game 5 of the 1956 World Series. Larsen had been pulled after giving up four runs in the second inning of Game 2, a 13-8 Dodgers victory. Did Stengel make a wise choice for that Game 5? All Larsen did was go out and pitch a perfect game.

Stengel was a comedian, full of wisdom and baseball sense. One of my favorite Stengel quotes is what he said to Mantle one day in practice at the Stadium. Stengel was telling the rookie how to field balls hit off the right field wall. Mantle looked at him in amazement as if he was thinking, "You played baseball here?" Stengel replied, "Do you think I've always been this old?"

Joe Torre was another odd choice to manage the Yankees. But like Stengel, he too had immediate success, winning the Series in the genesis of his years wearing pinstripes and then winning three of the next four. Torre led the Yankees to the post season every year he managed the club. He had a calm demeanor and treated his players with respect.

Although quite different than Steinbrenner, he knew how to respond to The Boss better than any of his predecessors. After an outstanding career as a player he had limited success managing the Mets, Braves, and Cardinals. His .605 winning percentage with the Yankees is one of the best for any manager on any team. He also managed the Dodgers for three years before going into administrative work with Major League Baseball. He was deserving of his 2014 entry in the Hall of Fame.

Another favorite Yankee is Michael Joseph Sheehy, better known as "Big Pete" to the hundreds of Yankees who wore the pinstripes that he cleaned, ironed, and hung in their lockers. The home clubhouse at the old Yankee Stadium was named for him, and there was also a plaque in the dugout that read, "Pete Sheehy, 1927–85, Keeper of the Pinstripes."

When I was a boy and my dad took me to games, I would always approach the coach and inquire about being the bat boy. If I weren't playing, I would do anything to be near the players at a baseball game. That's why I like Sheehy so much. He was that guy, beginning at age 17, and spending the rest of his life among the greatest players in baseball. The Yankees won 21 World Series titles and eight additional American League pennants during Sheehy's tenure. He was there with the great ones, beginning with Ruth and Gehrig and continuing to Don Mattingly's 1985

MVP season. It was Sheehy who issued the number 7 to Mantle after he was recalled from Kansas City so the Mick could get a new start rather than being pressed with number 6. There was mutual affection between the players and Sheehy.

Tony Morante is another non-playing Yankee who has a significant part in the story of the Yankees. For years, he has been giving tours of Yankee Stadium. His enthusiasm and knowledge of the team have endeared him to thousands who have walked with him in Monument Park and sat down in the Yankees dugout. He is easy to like and has a contagious spirit about the team he and I love. If I ever make it to New York again, I want him to lead me around the new Stadium.

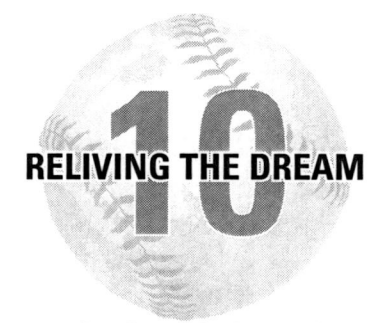

RELIVING THE DREAM

Can I come back again?

—Shoeless Joe Jackson

MY VISIT TO Yankee Stadium was a dream-come-true kind of day. June 22, 2005, is a day I will always remember. The game ended too soon. It was hard to leave. I didn't want to leave. I wasn't ready to leave. They made me leave.

Like Joe Jackson, I couldn't wait to return, and like Shoeless Joe, I wanted some of my friends to come along and enjoy the fun. I began thinking about the next time and if it would be at The House that Ruth Built or the new stadium across the street.

Going back to the field of my dreams almost happened in 2005, much sooner than I could have even imagined. The opportunity came during the American League Division Series, no less, but unfortunately, there was no *déjà vu*.

I got a call on Thursday, just two days before I was supposed to fly to Albany. The call was from Kerry Morris who informed me that one of the Christians in Albany worked for a company that had purchased tickets for Friday's game; the business associates had to cancel, and the tickets were available at no charge to me if I could get to New York that night. Bev was going with me on this trip, and if we could have changed our reservations, we would have been sitting in one of the luxury suites at the Stadium.

Talk about excitement. The Yankees played in October nearly every year until I was ten, and in 2005, they were in the playoffs for the eleventh straight year. I was given the chance to watch my favorite team, in October, at Yankee Stadium. Should I go? Could I go? Yes seemed to be the right answer, but there was a lot to consider. I had teaching assignments and exams to give that Friday, so I had to talk to my Dean. Both he and the Institute's President encouraged me to go. When I told my students, they were excited, and even offered to skip the exam just so Bev and I could go to the game. Typical.

The next and more important consideration involved money. I called the airlines and was told I could move the flight up one day and fly into LaGuardia Field. It would cost $130.00 for each passenger, just to change the reservations, and we would also have to pay the difference in airfare, which would be $350–400 each. I didn't have that much money, and I couldn't charge it on a credit card, especially after all I had spent on the trip in June. So we kept things as planned and flew to Albany on Saturday afternoon. Now, years later as I reflect on what might have happened, I say to myself, "Really? Did I really do that?" Good thing my dream had already come true four months earlier.

My son-in-law Jonathan Towell did take Lori to Atlanta in July for a surprise anniversary gift, no doubt one of the best gifts she had ever received. She got an autograph from Chipper Jones, her favorite player on her favorite team at her favorite ball field. Her dream came true after mine, but she didn't have to wait as long as I did. Am I jealous? Not at all. I got to go to New York and see the Yankees. I think I got the better deal.

In August, my son Josh's friend Robert Meyer got married in his hometown of Castle Rock, a few miles south of Denver. Josh and his wife Kyleen were about to begin their first year teaching at a school in Houston, and they had to be back on a Monday morning, two days after the wedding. I suggested they fly to Lubbock, then we would drive them to Colorado, and they could fly back from Denver on Sunday. It was a good plan, and it turned out to be a special time for all of us. We enjoyed the drive, and I had a few days to visit with family in Colorado.

There was another positive to the trip. I got to watch the Colorado Rockies play at Coors Field. Robert was eleven when the new franchise began playing in 1993, and he's been cheering for the team ever since. He treated his groomsmen and a few other friends to a game the night before his wedding. There was an extra ticket, and I got to go. It was a privilege to talk baseball throughout the game with Josh, Robert, and their friends. We got there early, so I did my usual thing of walking around the bleachers, waiting in the outfield seats for batting practice home runs, visiting the gift shop, and buying a hot dog. I knew the game was about to begin when we were invited to stand for the national anthem.

I still hadn't returned to my seat when the first pitch was thrown. It was a strike, but I didn't know it until I saw the light under "S" on one of the scoreboards. I was surprised at the crowd's meager reaction, which was not what I experienced with every strike thrown by Yankees pitchers the day I was at the Stadium. I am grateful to have been raised in Colorado, and I still like the Broncos, but I have to say, the hot dogs, the fans, and the overall atmosphere were much better in New York.

While Bev and I were in Albany, Kerry and his wife Alice offered to take us to Cooperstown, home to The National Baseball Hall of Fame and Museum. On the way, we saw part of the beauty that goes with the fall season in the northeast. It had rained every day we had been in Albany, but the rain stopped that day, and it was clear. The

Dreams Do Come True: A Lifelong Yankees Fan Visits the Stadium

trees were vibrant with fall colors, and the hills seemed to be alive with music. Cooperstown is a small, quaint village near Lake Otsego, surrounded by hills and full of breathtaking beauty. Bev loved the scenery, and I did too. But I wanted to see other things and found them inside the orange-bricked building that holds endless baseball memories. Many say Abner Doubleday began the game of baseball here in 1839. He couldn't have chosen a better place. Yankee Stadium is a beautiful work of man, but this area and all of its beauty are the works of God.

Visiting the museum was magnificent, far better than I had imagined. I wanted to look at every picture and read every piece of information displayed throughout the building. I lingered through the exhibits and breathed deeply. With all the treasures I saw and all the memories they triggered, it was hard to believe that I was really there. I took pictures and more pictures. I reminisced and reminisced some more. I am not a museum-going kind of person, but this was different. I wasn't sure if I was a ten-year-old boy or a 51-year-old man, but it didn't matter. It was all good.

*The author and his wife Bev in front of the Baseball Hall
of Fame and Museum in Cooperstown, New York*

Bev and Alice didn't stay long. They took the Morris's grandson for a walk and enjoyed the fresh, fall air and the beauty surrounding the town. I stayed a long time, not wanting to leave but knowing I had to. Down the street from the museum were businesses catering to baseball fans. I bought several souvenirs, and then Kerry and I decided to go to Doubleday Field. Although the bases were ninety feet apart, there was something extra large and wonderful about that diamond. I wanted to get on the grass and play catch.

Following our stay in Albany, we got together for a few days with our friends Mike and Nancy Mullen who live in Fall River, Massachusetts. One day, they took Bev and me to see Boston. How I wish we would have had another day or two. Of course Mike, a proud citizen of Red Sox nation, wanted me to see Fenway Park. I, too, was delighted to be there.

We took the tour of one of the oldest and most beloved ball fields in professional sports. Our guide was great. He was a crusty old veteran who loved the Sox and, of course, didn't like the Yankees. I tried to be polite and keep quiet, which I did, except for a few comments that only the few that were seated beside me could hear. Since it was raining, the tour was brief and involved more sitting than walking. We sat in the bleachers down the third base line and listened to many stories told by our guide. We weren't far from the place where Graig Nettles grabbed Yastrzemski's fly ball for the final out of the 1978 playoff game. I wanted to mention that event, or at least say that the pitcher who got the Red Sox captain out was from my hometown. But I remained quiet and respectful.

I was delighted to hear stories about The Green Monster, or "The Monstuh" as he called it, and the huge scoreboard. I had a big smile as he explained why Bostonians now refer to the dents on the wall as dimples. Again I kept quiet, but I really wanted to shout, "Hooray for Bucky Dent." There were other jabs taken at the Yankees, like the Yankees' fan, sleeping in right centerfield, who was hit on the head by a

Ted Williams' homer, believed to be the longest one ever hit at Fenway. I wanted to ask, "Why didn't a Red Sox fan reach out and catch it?" or, "Were there any Red Sox fans there that day?"

We were able to go up on the Monster and sit at one of the tables. The tour was enjoyable. Unfortunately we couldn't go down on the field or sit in the dugout because remodeling had begun the week before when the Sox were eliminated from the postseason. I knew I was in a place rich with baseball history, and I enjoyed every minute of it. So did Bev, who instantly became a Red Sox fan, simply because she fell in love with Fenway Park.

We enjoyed the gift shop across from the field. I bought a miniature bat, pin, and a few other things to add to my collection. In spite of the rain, it was a really good day.

After the White Sox won the Series, there would be no more games until Spring Training and the World Baseball Classic in March. Like other years, I was expecting a long, cold, lonely winter, but I knew when spring came again, the Yankees would be tied for first with only 162 games to play. I hoped for another postseason appearance for the Yankees, which would make 12 straight years. If that happened they would need only eleven wins in October to have their 27th championship.

Hope returns every spring, and baseball fans begin to dream again.

During the winter, I eagerly awaited the outcome of the baseball writers' votes to know if Goose Gossage was elected to the Hall of Fame. He wasn't, but Bruce Sutter was. Both were among the best relievers of their time, Sutter having nine outstanding seasons in a 12-year career while Gossage had 12 seasons of dominance in his 22 years in the majors. Both had one World Series ring. Only one would be enshrined in the summer of 2006. It made me wonder.

Every spring rolls around with thoughts of baseball on my mind. It's automatic. It happened when I lived in Brazil, even though I never watched any games and rarely read about them. Excitement is abundant at the beginning of the season because I know the Yankees will be playing with pride, wearing pinstripes at Yankee Stadium.

The 2006 season began for the Yankees with a six-game West Coast road trip. After winning just two games, they arrived in New York for their home opener against the Kansas City Royals. On the morning of April 11, I had seen Billy Crystal on one of the early morning TV programs and guessed that he would be at The Stadium for the afternoon game. I went to class, thinking of revisiting the monuments and walking around the Stadium. I dismissed class at noon (1:00 Eastern time), and when I looked at the clock, I thought the national anthem was being sung. I remembered talking to Lori at that same time just ten months earlier.

I rushed to my office, got connected to the internet, and was seated comfortably by the time the Yankees came to bat. The Royals had gone down in order in the top of the first. Jason Giambi launched a 3-run homer in the bottom half of the inning, and I was on my feet again (alone, of course; not many southerners cheer for the Yankees).

The Yankees allowed a run in the second, got it back in the third, then the Royals tied it in the fourth and took the lead in the sixth. In the bottom of the eighth, trailing 7-6, the captain Derek Jeter blasted a home run with two on to take a 9-7 lead. Mariano Rivera came in for the ninth, and despite giving up a single and hitting a batter, it was only a matter of time before the Yankees won. I knew the fans were hearing Frank Sinatra's version of "New York, New York." Liza Minnell's version was not heard that day.

For the 14th time in 15 years, the Yankees won their home opener. I was there, again, but only electronically. I wanted to be there to take it all in, to share the excitement of victory, to see the fans high-fiving each other, to slowly leave the seating area, and, of course, to grab a few drinking cups on my way out.

I made one trip to Yankee Stadium. It was just one, and I will never be the same. During the next three years, every game that was played there was a game I relived the fulfilling of my dream and wished I were there again. I have similar feelings like I had the day our family went fishing at a lake in the mountains. I was about ten, and I caught my first trout. Afterwards, I asked, "Dad, what's the limit?" Then, as now, I wanted more than just another one; I wanted as much as I could get.

What a life for a baseball fan. For fans of the New York Yankees, hopes and dreams do come true. I'm saying, "Go Yankees!"

Yankee Baseball after June 22, 2005

	W	L	Pct.	GB
xNew York	95	67	.586	—
yBoston	95	67	.586	—
Toronto	80	82	.494	15
Baltimore	74	88	.457	21
Tampa Bay	67	95	.414	28

x, clinched division title
y, clinched wildcard

What a finish. After losing to the Rays on June 22 and again the next night, the Yankees dropped to 37-35, just two games above .500. They trailed the division leading Orioles by five games, were four and one-half games behind the Red Sox, and were only one-half game ahead of the fourth place Blue Jays. The American League East, the toughest division in baseball, had four teams in a close race as the first half of the season was drawing to a close.

I knew then what everyone else knew: the Yankees offense could produce runs, lots of runs, but the pitching had to stop giving up so many. There would be winning and losing streaks the rest of the way, but the pitching finally came together, and the Yankees finished strong. Not until the penultimate day of the season, a Saturday when Randy Johnson pitched superbly and beat the Red Sox, was it certain that New York would make the playoffs. Up to that point, it wasn't clear who would win the division or even the wild card. It was tense. It was the way September baseball ought to be.

The Yankees finished September with a 19-9 record. When it meant the most, they went 15-3 before the final series in Boston, where they needed just one win, and got it, to earn a spot in the playoffs. The Yankees won the season series with their rivals from Beantown, 10-9, which secured the division title. The Red Sox backed into the playoffs on the final day of the season by beating the Yankees and watching Cleveland lose for the third straight day. I was disappointed in Cleveland (there's a statement that has been made more than a few times) because I wanted the Indians in and the Red Sox out. After the Aaron Boone home run in Game 7 of the 2003 ALCS and the famous

Red Sox comeback of 2004, I didn't want to think about another series between the two.

New York had to travel to Anaheim for the division series' first two games. Like the Red Sox, the Angels' record was identical to New York's, but unlike the Red Sox, the Angels had a better record against the Yankees, winning six of ten games during the regular season and gaining home field advantage.

In Game 1, played on October 4th, Robinson Cano hit a two-out, three-run double in the first inning and the Yankees never trailed. Mike Mussina pitched into the sixth inning without giving up a run. Mariano Rivera allowed a run in the ninth but got the save in the 4-2 victory.

The Los Angeles Angels of Anaheim came back to win Game 2 by a 5-3 score. Cano had another run-scoring, first inning double to give New York the early lead, but two Yankee errors led to three unearned runs, and the series was tied as the teams headed for Yankee Stadium.

Randy Johnson was the Game 3 starter at The Stadium, the one I would have attended if I had had an extra thousand bucks just waiting to be spent. I was hoping for another big game in October by The Unit, but he didn't have his best stuff that night. He pitched similar to the way he did the night before I saw the Yankees play in June, giving up five runs on nine hits in only three innings of work. The Yankees came back, however, and took a 6-5 lead into the sixth inning, only to lose it for second game in a row as the bullpen allowed six runs in an 11-7 defeat.

Our flight to Albany was on Saturday, October 8. Rain was in the forecast for most of the northeastern United States. There was a downpour as we switched planes in Philadelphia, and it hadn't let up any by the time we arrived in the Empire State's capital city. We were met at the airport by Kerry and Alice who informed us that Game 4 had been postponed.

The Yankees won the next day, 3-2. Shawn Chacon from my home state, one of the Yankees midseason pickups that strengthened their pitching staff, kept the game close, giving up two runs before being pulled in the seventh. After the singing of "God Bless America" and "Take Me Out to the Ball Game," the Yankees took a 3-2 lead with runs coming on a pinch hit single by Ruben Sierra and Derek Jeter's fielder's choice ground out. Rivera came in for a six-out save, and the series was knotted at two games apiece. I was excited watching the final innings in our hotel room after the evening worship assembly. I didn't preach a short sermon that night, but I had considered doing so.

When we left for dinner and church on Monday night, October 10, I was predicting a Game 5 Yankees victory, as in, "Ball game over. Division series over. Yankees win. Theeeeeeeeee Yankees Win!" But the words didn't come out of John Sterling's mouth; the final score from the west coast was Angels 5, Yankees 3.

I was disappointed with the loss and the early end of the season, but I had the privilege to be in New York and preach about God's grace and His love for people. There was no disappointment in that. The Yankees lost their final game that year (the "you can't win 'em all" comment I heard often as a youth came to mind), and not because of a curse, a bad call, a goat, or fan interference. Plain and simple, the Yankees were outplayed, outscored, and out of games until April 3, 2006.

If there was any consolation, it was that earlier in the week, Boston had been swept by Chicago, and it was possible that for the fifth year in a row the team to eliminate the Yankees would go on to win the Series. The White Sox, however, were just too good for both the Angels and the Houston Astros. This Chicago team won the World Series for only the third time in their history, and the first since 1917.

REFLECTIONS ON MY CUP OF COFFEE

"For once I can touch what my heart used to dream of"

—Ron Miller and Orlando Murden

I DRINK MORE coffee then I used to. Probably more than I need to, even though most of it is decaf. When I think of major leaguers as coffee drinkers (Joe DiMaggio was known to have been one), there are a few who have drunk deeply and often; they have made it into the Hall of Fame. There are also those who had a September call up and only watched a few games from the dugout, but even if they only got a sip, they remember it forever.

For nearly ten years, I have touched what used to be my dream. It was just a taste, but it is a memory I will treasure forever.

Since 2005 when I made two trips to New York and visited two of baseball's greatest buildings—Yankee Stadium and the Hall of Fame—I have experienced some of the saddest moments in my life but have also enjoyed some of the best times in life. There have been empty Octobers for the Yankees and their fans, deaths in the Yankees family, destruction of a New York landmark and the opening of a new Stadium for the dreams of others to come true, six former Yankees entering Cooperstown, and another World Series title. Besides these occurrences, there has been an opening day every year, when hope and excitement begin all over again.

The Yankees won the AL East Division in 2006 and earned a spot in the playoffs as the Wild Card team in 2007, but they managed to win only one game in October both years. Joe Torre's contract was up for renewal after the 2007 campaign, but he did not accept the team's offer to remain as manager. Former Yankee catcher and coach Joe Girardi replaced Torre as the Yankee skipper and announced he would wear Number 27, indicating his intention to manage New York to its 27th championship. It didn't happen in 2008. The Yankees didn't even make it to the postseason in the final year that games were played at the field of my dreams.

Our family welcomed a new member in 2007 when our youngest Daniel married Maggie Jones. She is from Arkansas, and most of her family and friends like the

Cardinals. I am trying to convince her that her favorite American League team should be the Yankees.

During the summer of 2008, cancer took the life of Bobby Ray Murcer. The former player and broadcaster, one of the most beloved Yankees, breathed his last on July 12 after a 19-month fight with brain cancer. He endeared himself to me after his phone call on the day I was at The Stadium, but I was already a fan, from his beginning days as a player and throughout his career, both on the field and in the press box. He was only 62. His autobiography, released just weeks before his death, is touching and inspirational. I read it in seven days. Our birthdays were just one day and eight years apart.

Two weeks and a day after Murcer's death, his friend and teammate (and my favorite Colorado athlete) Richard Michael "Goose" Gossage was finally inducted into the Baseball Hall of Fame. I was 54 years old that summer, and the guy who wore Number 54 was being enshrined at Cooperstown. I had had foot surgery the day before, but I watched his acceptance speech and listened with pride to every word he said. As he expressed gratitude to those who helped him along the way, mentioned setbacks that might have stopped his path to success, and reflected on high points in his career, I was filled with memories, as if I had walked beside him throughout his life. The only things we have in common are Colorado and the Yankees, but it is the latter that connects us together.

Other recent additions to the Hall, players who have worn pinstripes, are Joe Gordon and Rickey Henderson, both in 2009, and Randy Johnson in 2015. In addition, owner Jacob Ruppert (2013) and manager Joe Torre (2014) now have plaques in the national baseball museum.

George Michael Steinbrenner III also deserves a place in Cooperstown. The longtime owner was at the center of the Yankees return to baseball power, both on the field and in the financial marketplace. The Yankees won seven championships during his reign. He and his group purchased the team for $10 million and turned it into an empire worth more than $2 billion. The Boss passed away on July 13, 2010, at the age of 80. In his final October, the Yankees won another World Series title. Actually, it was on November 4, 2009, when the Yankees beat Philadelphia in Game 6 to earn their 27th crown.

There were significant events in my life in 2008. I had a one-year experiment with Fantasy Baseball, playing in a league with Josh, Jonathan, and several of their friends from their college days. They enjoyed it much more than I did. I had surgery that year to ease the pain and correct the deformity caused by two flat feet. (No wonder I was called "Turtle Man" by my friends and teammates who laughed at me for always finishing last in wind sprints.) My dad died that summer, and memories of him hitting pop flies and watching my games filled my mind. My favorite events were the births of our first two grandchildren, Abigail Bontrager Towell and Aidan Patrick Bontrager. If rounding the bases after a home run—which I did a few times playing slow-pitch softball—is a moment of ecstasy, having grandchildren is about ten times better.

I have read more than fifty books about baseball since my day at Yankee Stadium. It never grows old reading about Mantle and his teammates, about other Yankee teams and their successes, and about baseball history. "Baseball," in the words of Terrence Mann, "reminds us of all that once was good and could be again."

The new stadium was ready for the 2009 season, and the Yankees were again the best in baseball, culminating their inaugural year in the new house with their 27th championship by defeating the Philadelphia Phillies. It was just like the 1923 team that won it all in the first season at the old stadium and almost like the 1976 team, which went to the Series but lost to the Reds in the initial campaign after the renovation.

Ron Bontrager

*The author is all smiles after the Yankees
won the 2009 World Series*

I am certain there were many discussions regarding what
to do with The House that Ruth Built. The final decision
was to tear it down and leave nothing of baseball's most
famous building. That broke the hearts of many Yankee fans
whose dream never came true. The vacant Yankee Stadium

stood tall but empty during 2009 while the Yankees won the most games in Major League Baseball, then added 11 more wins in October to win the Series for the first time in nine years. Joe Girardi changed his uniform to Number 28.

The Stadium was home to so many greats, like Ruth, Gehrig, Dickey, DiMaggio, Berra, Rizzuto, Ford, Mantle, and Munson, and it proudly displayed the 26 banners of the championship teams that played there. While the 2009 Yankees played across the street, the former field and all its glory remained, as if the previous inhabitants were watching and waiting for another championship before the demolition work would begin.

Since the completion of the 2009 season, I have had five more surgeries (fusion in my neck, valve replacement in my heart and another heart procedure, and two more cuts on my right foot), I cried as I watched my mom take her final breath, and I was saddened again when my father-in-law died. Bev and I decided to move from the house where we finished raising our three children, which had become home to Bev's dad during his final seven years. The move necessitated plans for a new baseball room, and it now holds most of my books, pictures, and other baseball possessions.

We have rejoiced at the birth of three more grandchildren. I'm a proud PapaBon to Lydia Joy Towell, Kian Robert Bontrager, and Caleb Michael Bontrager. I talk to my grandchildren about baseball and will be playing catch with them as often as they want to, and I will tell them about the Yankees. Who knows, maybe one of them will become a Yankees fan. Since their parents are devoted to the Braves and Astros, that may be an impossible dream, but I've had one of those before, and it turned out better than I imagined.

The Stadium I visited will always be more important to me than the new one. I would be happy to go to the new one, and I am certain that the little boy in me would come out again, but I already experienced the joy of my dream coming true. I want to travel to New York again, with Bev, our children and in-laws, and our grandchildren, and if we do, we will go to a Yankees game at the field across the street from the famous site of so much Yankee history. Is that my next dream? No, the one that came true in 2005 was good enough, and the memories are still special. Anything else would be just gravy.

Yogi Berra made the memorable comment, "It ain't over 'til it's over." As for the Stadium of my dreams, 'til has come.

During the Yankees recent return to greatness, which began in 1995 with their first postseason appearance in 14 years, Jorge Posado, Andy Pettitte, Mariano Rivera, and Derek Jeter played significant roles in their success from 1996 through 2014. Known as "The Core Four," they contributed to 16 years of postseason games, 13 division championships, seven World Series appearances, and five titles.

The Yankees never had a losing record with those four on the roster.

Posada played 15 seasons in pinstripes, ending his career with 275 home runs. When he announced his retirement on January 24, 2012, he said, "I played baseball for the New York Yankees, and that was all I could think of and dream of when I was a little kid. I was able to live my dream, to play baseball for the best sports franchise in the world. Playing for the New York Yankees was an honor. I could never wear another uniform. I will forever be a Yankee."

Pettitte won 219 games while pitching for New York. He won 37 more during three years with his hometown Houston Astros. He retired after the 2010 season but came back one year later and pitched two more seasons with the Yankees. One of the best games of his entire career was his last, on September 28, 2013, in Houston. He pitched a complete game, giving up just five hits in a 2-1 victory. It was his only complete game during the final six years of his career. His savvy, determination, and manager Girardi's approval gave him the necessary strength to finish what he started.

Rivera announced at the beginning of the 2013 season that it would be his last. The Sandman completed his 19-year-career with a record 652 saves. Most pitchers lose their competitive edge if the batter knows what's coming. The amazing part of his success is that he threw one pitch, and everyone who stepped to the plate against him knew it. He exited the Yankee Stadium playing field the same way he entered it the first time in 1995: with class, humility, and appreciation to be a Yankee.

Jeter retired after the 2014 season with 3,465 base hits in his 20 years of playing for the only team he ever wanted to play for. His final week was marked with never-to-be-forgotten moments. In his last game at The Stadium, he came to bat in the ninth with the score tied and a runner on second. His single scored the winning run, and the place erupted. It was as if the Yankees had just won their 28th championship. The celebration lasted a long time. Hollywood couldn't have scripted a better ending. Three days later, in the third inning at Fenway Park, he drove in a run with an infield single. It was his last career at bat. He had already been cheered by the Red Sox faithful, and they applauded again as he left a professional baseball field for the final time.

Jeter was to younger fans what Mickey Mantle was to me: the greatest player on the greatest team in baseball. We imitated their stances, wanted their number on our uniforms, and listened with respect when their names were announced by Bob Sheppard. When Jeter called it quits, like Mantle's retirement forty-six years earlier, an entire generation of baseball fans was shocked; all of a sudden, we grew old and our youth began to disappear.

Baseball players describe a brief time in the big leagues as their "cup of coffee." Mantle and Jeter had theirs, and many more. A biblical expression to describe joy, found for example in Psalm 23 about "The Good Shepherd," is "my cup runneth over."

Being a Yankees fan and visiting the Stadium, I had both cups.

REFERENCES

Preface

page 20, "Here Comes the Sun," lyrics by John Lennon and
Paul McCartney; ©EMI Music.

Chapter 1: Field of My Dreams

page 25, from the film *Field of Dreams.*
page 30, Gossage & Pate, *The Goose is Loose* 23–24.

Chapter 2: Going Home

page 41, Psalm 126:1, taken from the NEW AMERICAN
STANDARD BIBLE®, Copyright© 1960, 1962,
1963, 1968, 1971, 1972, 1973, 1975, 1977, 1995 by The
Lockman Foundation. Used by permission.
page 44, Gossage & Pate, *The Goose is Loose* 24.
page 44, comment by Maddox in Angell's *Game Time* 348.

Chapter 3: There is Crying in Baseball

page 57, Torre & Verducci, *Chasing the Dream* 227.
page 58, Torre & Verducci, *Chasing the Dream* 7.
page 58, Torre & Verducci, *Chasing the Dream* 225–26
page 58, Torre & Verducci, *Chasing the Dream* 227

Chapter 4: Always a Yankee

page 79, Torre & Verducci, *Chasing the Dream* 310
pages 88–90, "Baseball Is," by Greg Hall©

Chapter 5: Team October

page 95, Berra, *What Time is It?*156
page 103, Gallagher & LeConte, *The Yankee Encyclopedia* 545.
page 104, comment by Berra in Liederman's *Our Mickey* ix.
page 105, Berra, *What Time is It?*156.
page 105, Tullius, *I'd Rather be a Yankee* xv.
page 105, comment by Russo in Madden's *October Men* 38.

Chapter 6: New York, New York

page 111, "New York, New York," lyrics by Fred Ebb and
John Kander
page 120, Gossage & Pate, *The Goose is Loose* 156.

Chapter 7: Playing Center Field in Yankee Stadium

page 129, comment by Mantle on Mickey Mantle Day at Yankee Stadium, June 8, 1969.

page 140, Gelman, *Young Baseball Champions* 103.

page 143, "Centerfield," lyrics by John Fogerty; ©Warner Bros. Records

page 144, comment by Mantle in Tullius's, *I'd Rather Be a Yankee* 227.

Chapter 8: A Glorious Quest

page 147, "The Impossible Dream," lyrics by Joe Darion.

Chapter 9: Priceless!

page 166, "Casey at the Bat," by Ernest Lawrence Thayer.

Chapter 10: Reliving the Dream

page 179, from the film, *Field of Dreams*

Chapter 11: Reflections on My Cup of Coffee

page 195, "For Once in My life," lyrics by Ron Miller and Orlando Murden

RECOMMENDED READINGS

I HAVE READ many baseball books in my life, especially while riding a bike at the gym during the last 12 years. The bike never moved an inch, from the time I got on until the time I got off, but my knowledge of baseball went a long distance. Here are my favorites.

Aaron, Hank, and Lonnie Wheeler. *I Had a Hammer: The Hank Aaron Story*. New York: HarperCollins, 1991.

Alexander, Charles C. *Our Game: An American Baseball History*. New York: MJF, 1991.

Allen, Maury. *All Roads Lead to October*. New York: St. Martin's, 2001.

Alvarez, Mark, ed. *The Perfect Game*. Dallas: Taylor, 1993.

Anderson, Dave, et. al. *The New York Yankees Illustrated History*. New York: St. Martin's, 2002.

Angel, Roger. *Game Time: A Baseball Companion*. Orlando: Harvest, 2003.

—. *The Summer Game*. New York: Viking, 1971.

Barra, Allen. *Mickey and Willie: Mantle and Mays, The Parallel Lives of Baseball's Golden Age*. New York: Crown Archetype, 2013.

Bashe, Philip. *Dog Days: The New York Yankees' Fall from Grace and Return to Glory, 1964–1976*. New York: Random, 1994.

Berkow, Ira, and Jim Kaplan. *The Gospel According to Casey*. New York: St. Martin's, 1992.

Berra, Yogi. *The Yogi Book: I Really Didn't Say Everything I Said*. New York: Workman, 1998.

Berra, Yogi, and Dave Kaplan. *Ten Rings: My Championship Seasons*. New York: HarperCollins, 2003.

——. *What Time is It? You Mean Now? Advice for Life from the Zennest Master of them All*. New York: Simon & Schuster, 2002.

——. *When You Come to a Fork in the Road, Take It: Inspiration and Wisdom from One of Baseball's Greatest Heroes*. Waterville, ME: Thorndike, 2001.

Boston, Talmage. *1939: Baseball's Tipping Point*. Albany, TX: Bright Sky, 2005.

Bradley, Richard. *The Greatest Game: The Yankees, the Red Sox, and the Playoff Game of '78*. New York: Free Press, 2008.

Buckley, James, Jr. *Classic Ballparks*. New York: Barnes & Noble, 2005.

Burkard, Tom. *The Ultimate Mickey Mantle Trivia Book.* Secaucus, NJ: Citadel, 1997.

Castro, Tony. *Mickey Mantle: America's Prodigal Son.* Washington, DC: Potomac, 2002.

Clavin, Tom, and Danny Peary. *Roger Maris: Baseball's Reluctant Hero.* New York: Touchstone, 2010.

Creamer, Robert W. *Baseball in '41: A Celebration of the Best Baseball Season Ever—In the Year America Went to War.* New York: Viking Penguin, 1991.

Davis, Mac. *The Greatest in Baseball.* New York: Scholastic, 1962.

Epstein, Sam, and Beryl Epstein. *Baseball Hall of Fame: Stories of Champions.* New York: Scholastic, 1966.

Falkner, David. *The Last Hero: The Life of Mickey Mantle.* New York: Simon & Schuster, 1995.

Ford, Whitey, and Phil Pepe. *Few and Chosen.* Chicago: Triumph, 2001.

——. *Slick.* New York: Dell, 1987.

Frommer, Harvey. *A Yankee Century.* New York: Berkley, 2002.

Gallagher, Mark, and Neil Gallagher. *Mickey Mantle.* New York: Chelsea, 1991.

Gallagher, Mark, and Walter LeConte. *The Yankee Encyclopedia.* 6th ed. Champaign, IL: Sports, 2003.

Gehrig, Eleanor, and Joseph Durso. *My Luke and I.* New York: Signet, 1976.

Gelman, Steve. *Young Baseball Champions.* New York: Scholastic, 1966.

Golenbock, Peter. *Dynasty: The New York Yankees, 1949–1964.* Englewood Cliffs, NJ: Prentice-Hall, 1975.

Gossage, Richard, and Russ Pate. *The Goose is Loose.* New York: Ballantine, 2000.

Great Baseball Stories. New York: Crescent, 1990.

Green, Ron, Jr. *101 Reasons to Love the Yankees.* New York: Stewart, 2005.

Halberstam, David. *October 1964.* New York: Villard, 1994.

——. *Summer of 1949.* New York: Morrow, 1989.

——. *The Teammates: A Portrait of a Friendship.* New York: Hyperion, 2003.

Hamilton, Josh, and Tim Keown. *Beyond Belief: Finding the Strength to Comeback.* New York: Faith Words, 2008.

Hershiser, Orel, and Jerry B. Jenkins. *Out of the Blue.* New York: Charter, 1989.

Herskowitz, Mickey, Danny Mantle, and David Mantle. *Mickey Mantle: Stories and Memorabilia from a Lifetime with the Mick.* New York: Stewart, Tabori & Chang, 2006.

Honig, Donald. *Baseball When the Grass was Real.* Lincoln: U of Nebraska P, 1975.

——. *Mays, Mantle, Snider: A Celebration.* New York: Macmillan, 1987.

Hoppel, Joe, ed. *Baseball: 100 Years of The Modern Era: 1901–2000*. St. Louis: Sporting, 2001.

Houk, Ralph, and Robert W. Creamer. *Season of Glory*. New York: Pocket, 1988.

Kahn, Roger. *The Era, 1947–1957: When the Yankees, the Giants, and the Dodgers Ruled the World*. New York: Ticknor & Fields, 1993.

——. *October Men: Reggie Jackson, George Steinbrenner, Billy Martin, and the Yankees' Miraculous Finish in 1978*. Orlando: Harcourt, 2003.

Kahn, Roger, and Al Helfer, eds. *The Mutual Baseball Almanac*. Garden City, NY: Doubleday, 1954.

Kettman, Steve. *One Day at Fenway: A Day in the Life of Baseball in America*. New York: Atria, 2004.

Leavy, Jane. *The Last Boy: Mickey Mantle and the End of America's Childhood*. New York: HarperCollins, 2010.

Leventhal, Josh. *Take Me out to the Ball Park: An Illustrated Tour of Baseball Parks Past and Present*. New York: Black Dog, 2000.

——. *The World Series: An Illustrated Encyclopedia of the Fall Classic*. New York: Black Dog, 2001.

Liederman, Bill, and Maury Allen. *Our Mickey: Cherished Memories of an American Icon*. Chicago: Triumph, 2004.

Madden, Bill. *Pride of October: What it Was to Be Young and a Yankee*. New York: Werner, 2003.

Mantle, Meryln, et. al. *A Hero all His Life: A Memoir by the Mantle Family*. New York: HarperCollins, 1996.

Mantle, Mickey. *The Education of a Baseball Player*. New York: Pocket, 1969.

——. *The Quality of Courage*. New York: Bantam, 1964.

Mantle, Mickey, and Herb Gluck. *The Mick*. New York: Doubleday, 1985.

Mantle, Mickey, and Mickey Herskowitz. *All My Octobers*. New York: HarperCollins, 1994.

Mantle, Mickey, and Phil Pepe. *My Favorite Summer: 1956*. New York: Island, 1991.

Masin, Herman L. *How to Star in Baseball*. New York: Scholastic, 1960.

Meany, Tom, et. al. *The Magnificent Yankees*. New York: Barnes, 1952.

Morris, Jim, and Joel Engel. *The Rookie*. New York: Warner, 2001.

Murcer, Bobby, and Glen Waggoner. *Yankee for Life: My 40-Year Journey in Pinstripes*. New York: HarperCollins, 2008.

Neyer, Rob. *Rob Neyer's Big Book of Baseball Legends: The Truth, The Lies, and Everything Else*. New York: Fireside, 2008.

Nuttall, David S. *Mickey Mantle's Greatest Hits*. New York: SPI, 1998.

O'Connor, Ian. *The Captain: The Journey of Derek Jeter.* Boston: Mariner, 2011.

O'Neill, Paul, and Burton Rocks. *Me and My Dad.* New York: HarperCollins, 2003.

Plimpton, George, ed. *Home Run.* San Diego: Harcourt, 2001.

Reidenbaugh, Lowell. *Cooperstown: Baseball's Hall of Fame.* New York: Gramercy, 1999.

Ribowsky, Mark. *The Complete History of the Home Run.* New York: Citadel, 2003.

Richardson, Bobby. *The Bobby Richardson Story.* Old Tappan, NJ: Revell, 1965.

Ritter, Lawrence S. *The Glory of Their Times.* New York: Macmillan, 1966.

Rizzuto, Phil, and Tom Horton. *The October Twelve: Five Years of New York Yankee Glory, 1949–1953.* New York: Doherty, 1994.

Robinson, Ray, ed. *Baseball Stars of 1965.* New York: Pyramid, 1965.

Robinson, Ray, and Christopher Jennison. *Yankee Stadium: 75 Years of Drama, Glamor, and Glory.* New York: Penguin, 1998.

Ryan, Nolan, and Harvey Frommer. *Throwing Heat: The Autobiography of Nolan Ryan.* New York: Avon, 1990.

Schiffer, Don, ed. *World Series Encyclopedia.* New York: Nelson, 1961.

Schoor, Gene. *The Illustrated History of Mickey Mantle*. New York: Carroll & Graf, 1996.

Sherman, Joel. *The Birth of a Dynasty*. New York: Rodale, 2006.

Silverman, Al. *Yankee Colors: The Glory Years of the Mantle Era*. New York: HNA, 2009.

Siner, Howard. *Sweet Seasons: Baseball's Top Teams since 1920*. New York: Pharos, 1988.

Smith, Ken. *Baseball's Hall of Fame*. 11th rev. ed. New York: Grosset & Dunlap, 1981.

Smith, Robert. *Baseball in the Afternoon: Tales from a Bygone Era*. New York: Simon & Schuster, 1993.

———. *Baseball's Hall of Fame*. Rev. ed. New York: Bantam, 1973.

Stanton, Tom. *Hank Aaron and the Home Run that Changed America*. New York: HarperCollins, 2004.

Thorn, John. *A Century of Baseball Lore*. New York: Galahad, 1976.

Torre, Joe, and Tom Verducci. *Chasing the Dream*. New York: Bantam, 1997.

———. *The Yankee Years*. New York, Doubleday, 2009.

Tullius, John. *I'd Rather be a Yankee*. New York: Jove, 1986.

Tygiel, Jules. *The Great Experiment: Jackie Robinson and His Legacy*. Exp. ed. New York: Oxford UP, 1997.

———. *Past Time: Baseball as History*. Oxford: Oxford UP, 2000.

Vancil, Mark, and Mark Mandrake, eds. *Players in Pinstripes*. New York: Rare Air, 2004.

Weinberger, Miro, and Dan Riley, eds. *The Yankees Reader*. Boston: Houghton Miflin, 1991.

White, G. Edward. *Creating the National Pastime: Baseball Transforms Itself, 1903–1953*. Princeton: Princeton UP, 1996.

Will, George F. *Bunts*. New York: Simon & Schuster, 1999.

Wolfe, Rich. *For Yankee Fans Only*. Celebration, FL: Lone Wolfe, 2004.

CPSIA information can be obtained at www.ICGtesting.com
Printed in the USA
LVOW10s1456080716

495161LV00005B/10/P